The Disruptors: Data Science Leaders

Collective Biographies of Influential Leaders: Vol I

KATE STRACHNYI

ISBN-13: 978-1985855212
ISBN-10: 1985855216

Praise for *The Disruptors*

"Kate is a recognized contributor in the Data Science community and in her new book she holds your hand as you explore the careers of some of the most influential people in the field. Packed with fascinating stories, *The Disruptors* will both amaze and inspire you to build a successful data-driven career of your own."

**- Kirill Eremenko, CEO,
SuperDataScience**

"Kate has a zeal for exposing the inner workings of the various roles with the data professions. Let this book open your eyes to a whole new world of professional possibilities for the modern data worker."

**- Lillian Pierson P.E., Data
Strategist, Data-Mania, LLC**

"*The Disruptors* is a book that fills an important gap in today's landscape of data science books that all miss one important section. Namely, the one that answers the following question: now that you know all those technical concepts you learned from the book on Data Science, what should you do to become a great data scientist? Kate's book gives future data scientists ten excellent inspirations."

**- Andriy Burkov, Machine Learning
Team Leader, Gartner**

"Get ready for a guided tour through the dawn of the data science. Kate Strachnyi brings us stories and insights from ten of the discipline's pioneers. The collection helps us, data science beginners and veterans alike, to understand the history of the field and by extension, its future."

— **Brandon Rohrer, Data Scientist, Facebook**

"Kate's latest book continues in the tradition of her other great bodies of work, by providing a closer glimpse at the diversity of the budding data science landscape. Each person's unique story inspires and reminds us that you don't need a PhD to understand and leverage the power of data."

— **Jennifer Cooper, Marketing Analytics Leader and Data Science Evangelist**

"Kate Strachnyi has put together another must-read for aspiring and practicing data scientists alike. Want to learn how the leaders are disrupting with data science? Read this book!"

— **Matthew Mayo, Machine Learning Researcher & Editor at KDnuggets**

"Reading *The Disruptors: Data Science Leaders* is like taking a journey through the world of data science, from the perspective of people helping to invent the discipline. It's relaxing and inspiring, and the reader feels like they are having a conversation with each of the data science leaders."

— **James I. Howard, Chief Data Officer & Chief Privacy Officer**

"As someone who lives and breathes data, *The Disruptors* gave me chills. Any data lover will be enthralled reading the experience and trajectories of these influential members of the field."

- Kristen Kehrer, Founder,
Data Moves Me, LLC

"*The Disruptors* is a fun way to get to know the leaders in the Data Science community. The meandering path some of these brilliant people took to fall into Data Science almost feels like the field chose them. The book gives hope and inspiration for entrants to the field as well as advice for data scientists and business leaders. Great job Kate!"

- Nic Ryan, Principal Data Scientist,
DataFriends

"Kate Strachnyi does an excellent job in sharing interviews she conducted with well-known data scientists to gain insights on their unique journeys and their advice to fellow data scientists. This must-read offers so much to learn from the experiences of these professionals like how they started in data science, what their struggles were, their opinions of the field, and the amazing accomplishments they have had along the way."

- Megan Silvey, Founder,
Silvey Solutions

"As an aspiring data scientist, your path into the field does not have to be a lonely one. This book is a piece of its own and should be read by anybody who wants to learn more about Data Science. You will learn everything you need to know and be put onto the path of these data science leaders. Packed with insights and resources, I highly recommend this book to any data aspirants."

- Randy Lao,
Principal Data Scientist,

"*The Disruptors* provides much needed insight into the people behind the big data revolution. By diving deep into leaders' perspective, readers can gain not only a unique perspective not only on the big data revolution of years past but also an understanding of where the disruptions in the field will occur in the future. This is a fascinating and fun read for anyone in the field!"

**- Eric Weber, Cofounder,
Method Data Science**

"Data science is already too broad to define; data scientist is even broader. That is why as a working data scientist, I'm always curious about the projects that other data scientists work on and also their path to become successful leaders in this field. Therefore, reading this book is very refreshing and interesting. I learn in depth about where some of these leaders are coming from and their unique background. This book will be good read for anyone who is curious about data science and how various leaders in data science disrupt multiple industries."

**- Kevin Tran, Senior Data
Scientist, Stanford University**

"Beyond data science, these are the stories of the people who built a wave of disruptive technology. *The Disruptors* is a must read for insights on what it takes to be on the leading edge of the waves to come."

**- Vin Vashista, Founder & Chief Data Scientist,
V-Squared Data Strategy Consulting**

"These days, there is no shortage of people giving advice to data scientists or those who manage them. What is missing, however, is what you'll find in Strachnyi's book: valuable information straight from the mouths of data science leaders. The table of contents reads like a Who's Who of data science influencers so you can be sure that listening to what they have to say is well worth your time. If you are serious about truly understanding data science, this is one book that needs to be on your bookshelf."

- Mark Meloon, Data Scientist,
Service Now

"Kate has written a fascinating behind the scenes book on the motivations, interests and challenges faced by key data science figures. She also simultaneously provides a historical overview of how data science evolved over the years to become one of the most exciting fields of our time."

- Matt Corey, Author of *Data Scientist's Book
***of Quotes* and Director of Change Force**

DEDICATION & ACKNOWLEDGMENTS

Dedicated to my family, and to all that love data!

Thank you to everyone that has provided priceless feedback, suggestions, and encouragement for writing this book.

Thank you to the data science leaders for being generous with your time and for your patience with the writing and review process: Bernard Marr, Carla Gentry, Craig Brown, DJ Patil, Drew Conway, Kirk Borne, Mico Yuk, Monica Rogati, Natalie Evans Harris, and Vivian Zhang.

Thank you to the data science community for being so collaborative and letting me in to your network.

Thank you to my family for their love, patience, encouragement, and belief in my abilities.

FOREWORD BY TOM DAVENPORT

When data scientists first began to emerge in online companies like Google, Facebook, and LinkedIn in the first decade of the 21st century, they were a relatively homogenous group. They were almost all based in Silicon Valley, they worked for similar types of firms, they had prodigious amounts of education and intelligence, they did some combination of programming and analytical work, and they were primarily interested in creating new products or capabilities based on data and analytics. With a few exceptions, most were young and male.

Now, however—as this book perfectly illustrates—there is substantially more diversity among people who call themselves data scientists. The group of them profiled in this book is quite diverse in terms of gender, ethnicity, geography, professional backgrounds, and types of organizations with which they are affiliated.

They are also quite varied in terms of what they do as a "data scientist," which both makes the job more interesting and more difficult to classify. Some actually do data science, while others write, teach, or consult about it. Some work with complex big data, others are more focused on traditional business intelligence. Some are moving into artificial intelligence. Since there is no clear definition in the world about what constitutes a data scientist, we should expect to see this level of variance in what data scientists do.

That doesn't mean, however, that the data scientists that Strachnyi describes in this book don't have some things in common. Almost all, for example, seem a bit rebellious (or disruptive), which perhaps explains how they got into the pathbreaking field of data science early on. Their primary goal is not to preserve job security; instead, they wanted a challenge and to have impact in their jobs. Most have moved around a lot—across job types, companies, and industries. The majority of these data scientists don't work for large organizations anymore (although some worked for one of the largest organizations, the US government). There are lots of consultants in the bunch—a job, of course, with high levels of independence. If you're trying to hire and retain data scientists, the lesson from this book is that you are unlikely to hire people like them and then see them quietly do what you tell them to do for many years of job tenure.

Many of the data scientists in this book would like to see the job description change. They would prefer to see more clarity about the role and activities of data science. They'd like to see some standards for typical data science capabilities. As with physicians, they'd like an ethic of "first do no harm" in the job. Ironically, given the variation in their backgrounds, if there were strict standards for the job of data scientist, some might not qualify for it!

Data science can be both exciting and tedious. Although I had some qualms about writing a 2013 article in *Harvard Business Review* with DJ Patil calling data scientists "the sexiest job of the 21st century," these people are very appealing. They are clearly smart, very curious, devoted to doing good and interesting work, and dedicated to the profession of data-driven discovery. It's great that Kate Strachnyi has profiled such interesting individuals, and that in reading this book we get to see the mosaic of what constitutes data science in practice.

Thomas H. Davenport

Distinguished Professor, Babson College and Research Fellow, MIT

Author of *Competing on Analytics*, *Big Data @ Work*, and *The AI Advantage*.

INTRODUCTION

My name is Kate Strachnyi and I am obsessed with data science. I'm captivated by its potential to uncover hidden insights within the vast universe of information. I'm captivated by its ability to predict what we'll do tomorrow by analyzing what we've done in the past. But most importantly, I'm fascinated with the people behind the scenes; those who make this field more exciting each and every day: the data science community. The ambitious, inquisitive, and talented individuals who strive to continuously better themselves through learning and education. To that end, my ultimate goal is to provide value to this community by sharing key characteristics of some of most influential data science leaders.

I've received positive feedback from aspiring data scientists on my first book, *Journey to Data Scientist* – which provides key insights from more than twenty interviews, in which I asked leading data scientists questions about how they got started in the field and about their perspective on the future of the industry. The feedback I've received from those that found the book useful inspired me to write *The Disruptors: Data Science Leaders*.

WHY THIS BOOK? You are probably familiar with the term data science; it has the power to make informed predictions using data. The excitement in this field is creating interest across industries and pressure on businesses to get up to speed and capitalize on this thing called data. Data scientists are the practitioners of the field and are the heroes of this book.

Most data science books focus on technical details, theory, etc. Those books are valuable, and they provide an inordinate amount of useful, actionable ideas on how to use data science to make an impact. This book takes a different approach.

The goal was to find the brightest data scientists in the world and tell their stories. I am truly grateful for the time they've invested in making this book happen. The most challenging part of the process was selecting the data scientists (and getting them to commit to an hour-long call). I felt star-struck talking to people like DJ Patil, the first chief data scientist in the White House, or Bernard Marr, a famous business influencer. The fact that they were able to dedicate their time to this project shows how truly great this space is – the community is highly collaborative and generous.

It was a long and arduous process to select the ten individuals that you will hear from in this book. In fact, it was so difficult to choose, that a decision was made to make this book into a series which highlights ten individuals in each book.

Once the data scientist list was finalized, I spent a considerable amount of time researching their life stories and career trajectories. Unique questions were designed for each individual, and then the interview process commenced. The stories heard from these people are incredible and provide several opportunities to learn and be inspired. By telling their stories, I hope that current and future generations of data scientists will use them to learn, be inspired, and elevate the profession to higher levels.

WHO AM I? I am fascinated with the fast-changing and evolving field of data science, as well as the community. Getting to know these accomplished individuals better can help others learn about how this space was shaped and the capabilities of data science. I'm so passionate about talking to data scientists that I host Humans of Data Science on my Story by Data YouTube channel. There, I'm in the process of interviewing hundreds of data scientists from all over the world, in different industries, with different levels of expertise and backgrounds.

I am obsessed with data; specifically, data visualization, and I spend my free time visualizing anything I can get my hands on, including my running statistics, data on maternity leave across various countries, my credit card spend, etc.

Regardless of industry, location, or market maturity, data science can help businesses succeed. This is why it's important to learn from the people that have used the power of data science to make an impact on this world.

This book introduces the reader to 10 influential data scientists; learning about their lives, careers, experiences, as well as how they've come to the field of data science.

The Disruptors is intended for several sorts of readers:

- Aspiring data scientists

- Data scientists implementing solutions

- Business people that work with data scientists, manage data science projects, or invest in data science-related ventures

Join me in getting down and personal with some of the most influential leaders in the data science world to uncover the characteristics that make them 'The Disruptors'.

CONTENTS

BERNARD MARR

BUSINESS, TECHNOLOGY AND DATA EXPERT; FOUNDER AND CEO OF BERNARD MARR & CO

> "Data is changing our world and the way we live and work at an unprecedented rate."

Bernard Marr is a prolific writer, speaker, and consultant who is shaping the face of data science as the field evolves. Marr studied business, information management and engineering in Germany before he completed his masters at Cambridge University and Cranfield School of Management. Marr confesses that his career was focused on data from the very beginning. He began by working for and researching at Cambridge University. He continued working in the academic setting, serving as a research fellow for prestigious business schools. Eventually, he decided that building his own business was going to be his main focus.

While his publishing and social media work garners the most notice, Marr has owned his own consulting company, Bernard Marr & Co., for over twenty years. The company offers a variety of services that have strategy, business performance and data at their core. From strategic board level advice, to training and research, the company helps other businesses and government agencies create more intelligent strategies, use data more strategically, and leverage technologies such as artificial intelligence to drive business performance.

How did you get started in data science?

"When I did my dissertation at Cambridge University, one of the areas I was focusing on was how companies use data to inform decision making. I spent 10 years in academia doing research and teaching others how companies were using data. I was also able to do some consulting projects on the side, which allowed me to build up my own consulting portfolio."

Marr's clients have ranged from IT giants like Microsoft to the United Nations and NATO. If there is a leader in an industry, Marr has worked with them and their data, up to and including Walmart, Walgreens, Toyota, Mars, Cisco, and AstraZeneca.

Can you talk about some of your notable projects?

"These days, I feel lucky that I can pick and choose the things I work on; I've been exposed to amazing projects and fascinating companies. I work with both the cutting-edge companies like Google or IBM, and the incumbent companies such as Walmart or Shell, to get fascinating insights into what is possible as well as the key the challenges of transitioning a traditional company into more of a digital

company that uses data as a core asset.

The work with Walmart has been fascinating for me. They have a massive private data cloud of over 150 petabytes of data. One objective was to get more people to use this data to make better decisions. To that end, they've developed not only amazing user interfaces so people can access data but also the skills gap that often exists in companies. They developed the idea of 'Data Cafés,' which are physical coffee shops in their headquarters where people can have coffee and sit down with a data scientist or data translator to explore their questions and how to use the data and tools to help get insights. They showed people how to catch fish vs. give them fish. They now have many more people that are confident in using the data and they can come back to the Cafes if they have more questions. They were able to create a supportive environment."

Is data science only for the bigger/ more established companies?

"Data science can be relevant to any business. For example, there is this small, local London butcher shop that was skeptical of data science at first. We then looked at their strategic challenges. Your data strategy has to start with your business strategy. They were wondering how to get new customers, should they compete on prices, how to engage new customers, how to analyze customer footfall, etc. We installed simple sensors inside the store window to track overall footfall and measure how effective displays and promotions were with passing customers. This was possible because most people carry smartphones with them these days, which emit signals to find Wi-Fi and Bluetooth connections.

For the first time, the owners of the butcher shop can actually see how many people walked past the shop, how many stopped to look at displays/signs, and how many people came into the store. They learned that price wasn't key; it was mostly about engaging their customers.

One surprise that we uncovered was there was increased footfall traffic during the hours of 9pm-12am. This was due to two popular pubs being located on the same street. This led the butcher shop to experiment and start opening on Friday and Saturday nights, serving premium hot dogs and burgers to hungry folks making their way home after a few beers.

They took this a step further and used Google to uncover food trends and identified chorizo sausage and pulled-pork as two popular food items. They decided to add this to the menu and served it during their new late-night hours. These days, about 50% of their profits are coming from these late-night hours that they likely wouldn't even know about if not for data science. Any company can use data as an important asset."

An impactful author

In addition to Marr's successful consulting company, he is also an impactful author. His work is featured regularly in well-read magazines, and his books have been recognized as bestsellers. *"I always enjoyed writing books; I wanted to make a difference in the world. In academia, there is pressure to publish theoretical, academic-style papers. I decided that I can make a larger impact by writing books instead, which can be read by hundreds of thousands of people, or focus on publishing on Forbes, etc."*

Marr's 15+ books have been published internationally, garnering many awards. He has contributed columns to all major technology and news outlets. His works have appeared in The Wall Street Journal, The Guardian, and Forbes, among others. In addition to the well-known news outlets, Marr contributes leadership articles to many publications, such as HR Review, The Sun, and Financial Management.

Marr has written multiple books that serve to define and guide the evolution of data science. In addition to the countless articles and textbooks that Marr has written, he authored *The Intelligent Company* in 2010. Marr made the case for why business models are shifting. In this book, he advocates for the next generation of companies to use evidence-based management. Evidence-based management uses analytics and key performance indicators, along with a whole other host of data science functions, to help make decisions and bring competitive advantage to businesses. Although the book is now eight years old, it is still a practical guide that will identify problems and offer solutions for businesses swimming through large amounts of data.

Big Data was his seminal and best-selling work, published in 2015. In this book, Marr spoke to individuals trying find their way through the morass of information concerning big data. The book is another practical blueprint that does more than explain the theoretical underpinnings of big data as a concept. In this book, Marr lays out a five-step process that he calls the SMART model. The steps of this model explained in his book are as follows: start with strategy, measure metrics and data, apply analytics, report results, transform. Marr used real examples from his consulting work that show how these steps can be applied in real life.

Big Data in Practice followed closely after in 2016, and *Data Strategy* is the latest work by the author, hitting the shelves in 2017. Each of these works are full of information that show how data can be used to streamline and improve processes in the private as well as the public sector.

"My books are positioned as business books. I hope that I can demystify and explain things in ways that others can understand. I try to make it relevant to people in business and explain what data means, and provide examples and frameworks that help them do this more strategically. For me, it is about closing the gap between business and technology, and I come to it from a business perspective. It's about solving problems in business and society. I try to show what's possible and share best practices."

Who encouraged you early on in your career?

"Everyone you work with influences and encourages you in some way or another. When I was running industry networks, seeing how companies were struggling in practice with obtaining the right information and turning it into insights that was an inspiration for me. I've followed the work of Tom Davenport; he's been close to what I did for years. His book gave me lots of inspiration."

Are you working on any new books at the moment?

"I am in the process of writing a book on AI in Practice, following a similar model of my 'Big Data in Practice' book. The new book will be collection of case studies featuring AI giants like Google, Baidu, Alibaba, Amazon as well as many traditional brands to discuss how they are using AI to drive their business. I plan to also take a look at all different sectors and uncover how AI is used to drive business performance. The book is expected to publish in the next year."

Who is a data scientist?

Marr has written work defining what data scientists do, and a large part of his writing works to educate the public about this field. Marr points out that most people understand how data scientists somehow draw conclusions from large collections of data, but he also wants the public to gain an understanding of what tasks such work might include for the data scientist on a day-to-day basis.

A data scientist must, on a daily basis, understand the meaning behind data, understand the problem that is to be solved, and must leverage technical expertise to solve the problem. This can mean needing to fine-tune complex algorithms. Machine learning algorithms are constantly evolving, and this requires careful consideration as to which tool a data scientist uses.

Marr is aware that many people try to market themselves as data scientists to take advantage of lucrative salaries available to a small pool of qualified people. Marr cautions individuals against calling themselves data scientists when they lack the appropriate skills. He sees a data scientist as having experience beyond the academic realm and skills beyond Excel. He advocates for a data scientist having intangible skills. The data scientist must be able to bring interpretation and visualization to the data. This intangible skill requires a creativity that works within the context of the data collection.

"We don't have a definition of a data scientist at the moment. It frustrated me sometimes when data analysts called themselves data scientists. It's probably just human nature to want to capitalize on opportunities, since data science is one of the hottest areas in the job market right now. There's huge enthusiasm in this space, and it's a good thing. There's a perfect mix that can be created in a person that has the understanding of analytical skills, math and statistics skills, with computer science skills. It's a great foundation, then you throw creativity, business awareness, and strong communication skills into this mix, and you have a high-profile data scientist.

The challenge is that I often don't see all of these skills in one person. We have different roles, where data scientists work with data translators that have fewer math and stats skills but more business, communication, and creativity skills. This is a more realistic picture of what works really well in organizations."

Marr has been crucial in developing and defining the field of data science. Many of his articles detail the differences between traditional career fields and data science. Marr came up with his own definition of big data, defining the concept as "everything we do is increasingly leaving a digital trace (or data), which we (and others) can use and analyze.

Big Data therefore refers to that data being collected and our ability to make use of it. While we have always collected data in some form or fashion as long as humans have had language, today is different in two main ways. Data is collected in massive quantities and no longer has to be solely discrete numbers. Data is now collected from 'unstructured' pieces, such as pictures and voice recordings.

What would you change in the data science space?

"The field is super exciting, and it's a real privilege to be a part of this fourth industrial revolution. I would want more honesty within the field. It would be great to go beyond all the hype and hear the honest perspectives of the journeys and challenges companies face in data science. This honesty would help if organizations would admit to things not being easy and talk about the real challenges of getting the data, getting systems to speak to each other, etc. It would also be nice for

companies to be more transparent on the use of their data. It is potentially a threat to the data science field. Companies try to get away with too much and exploit customer data without their knowledge."

Advice those trying to hire data scientists

In addition to defining the field of data science, Marr gives advice for those seeking to hire a data scientist. Technical skills such as programming or producing analytics are crucial, but hiring solely on those skills can lead to a deficit of other skills on the team. The candidate needs to show that they have applied their skills in such a way as to concretely improve a business model. The candidate ideally has a portfolio of these types of experiences, along with a solidly scientific perspective. Communication skills are also a necessity for a good data scientist. A good candidate will also bring intangible skills to their work, like open-mindedness and creativity.

Whether your organization is able to field a data scientist or not, Marr recommends that every manager improve their own data science skills. This awareness of data science brings added value to the manager who can excel at more technical tasks. The manager should be able to explore what kinds of experiments might improve processes. The application of the scientific method should not be something relegated to high school science classes. Again, math and statistics rear their ugly heads. While a manager need not be an expert, a working knowledge of these fields will make the manager more versatile. Once a person can figure out how the numbers work, they should try to become versed in visualizing those numbers. Communicating and explaining the data to others is a crucial tool for managers and data scientists alike. Of course, the numbers alone do not paint the big picture. The manager should be able to grasp the problems and solutions hidden within the numbers.

Data and business influencer

Marr is a crucial influencer in the world of data. Recently recognized as one of the biggest influencers in the world of data science, Marr is also one of LinkedIn's top five business influencers. Marr boasts over 1.3 million followers on the LinkedIn platform, 130,000 Facebook fans and over 100,000 Twitter followers. He currently gains about 1,000 new followers each day.

Marr stays busy giving frequent interviews, and, as recently as April 2018, Marr was jumping into the mix to explain how big data helps cull through information, leaving leaders like CFOs in a better position to focus on growing their companies. According to Marr, the traditional role of the CFO should broaden now that AI can handle some of the tedious work involved in financial data processing.

The prolific, practical, and precise work of Bernard Marr recently earned the author a European Data Hero Award. Marr is more than deserving of the honor, and millions will be watching him as he continues to shape the field of data science.

In addition to his hectic work schedule, Marr stays busy with his three kids, 12, 10, and 6, a girl and two younger boys.

CARLA GENTRY

OWNER AND DATA SCIENTIST AT ANALYTICAL
SOLUTION

"A data scientist does not simply collect and report
on data, but also looks at it from many angles,
determines what it means, then recommends ways
to apply the data."

A self-professed 'data nerd' Carla Gentry is the owner and data scientist of Analytical Solution. Gentry, a mathematician and economist, has helped companies by bringing everything she has learned about data, software and other analytical solutions to enable them to uncover the insights available for effective business decision. She acts as a liaison between technology and the business, to make sense of complicated data and to drive profits.

Gentry is an acknowledged influencer and subject matter expert in the field of advanced analytics and data science. She spends her time as a private contractor for many companies, including, but not limited to, Rivo Software LTD, PBA Health, Disney Media Burbank CA, Computer Systems Institute, Data Science Central with Vincent Granville, Deloitte, Talent Analytic, Corp., and SAMTEC Inc.

With over two decades of professional experience, being called a 'data nerd' is a badge of courage for this curious mathematician/economist. As Gentry said in her interview, *"I'm in the data science field for the passion."*

Rocky road to data scientist

Gentry's story is truly inspirational. She had a rough start when she made a decision to drop out of high school two weeks into the 11th grade, surprising her friends and family, as she'd been attending advanced classes and schools for the gifted her whole life. Things didn't get easier when she finally decided to end an abusive marriage of 5 years after having 2 kids (Keith and Johnathon). She worked as a clerk in a convenience store and later held a position with Orkin Pest Control. Her life was improving; however, Gentry wasn't satisfied.

In the early 1990s, she decided to enroll in college and told her children that they'd have to make some sacrifices in the hopes of a better future. She worked part-time throughout her education and worked even harder in school. She graduated with a Bachelor's of Science in Mathematics and Economics.

Her life changes really paid off. She's now held several positions including junior analyst, senior analyst, marketing information manager, director, and business owner. She is the role model for resilience and persistence.

Advice to female data scientists

Her advice to aspiring female data scientists was to the point — *"Stand your ground, be confident in yourself, find mentors, keep going, and keep learning. You will find the perfect fit for you as long as you continue to believe in yourself and your abilities."* She strongly believes that in order to incorporate more females into this field, the change has to start from the top.

Education and early career

Gentry has multiple degrees in mathematics and economics from the University of Tennessee, where she graduated top of her class while raising her two boys as a single mom. She believes data scientists are inquisitive: exploring, asking questions, doing 'what if' analyses, questioning existing assumptions and processes. Armed with data and analytical results, a top-tier data scientist will then communicate informed conclusions and recommendations across an organization.

Gentry has worked with structured and unstructured data as well as programmers, developers, architects, scrum masters, and other data scientists, and she can tell you, they don't all think alike. A data scientist could be a statistician, but a statistician may not be completely ready to take on the role of data scientist, and the same goes for all the above titles as well.

Thoughts on data science ethics? How can we get to a point where we have a code of ethics?

"We need some sort of data science creed, a data scientist do no harm; just like the doctors have. It would have to be self-created in the industry. Something that's like

a pledge, maybe a non-profit. Create unbiased algorithms. When you are building algorithms, it isn't a game, this will impact people's lives. Things like autonomous cars; they need to be continuously improving these systems. There is no course or professor that can teach data science; unless they have experience working for 2 decades with imperfect data with companies."

Gentry values privacy and the need to be clear with clients and customers about where you are going to use their data, for what purposes, and how it might impact them (if at all). The General Data Protection Regulation (GDPR), a regulation issued in the European Union (EU) is focused on data protection and privacy for all individuals within the EU. It aims primarily to give control to individuals over their personal data and to simplify the regulatory environment for international business by unifying the regulation within the EU. GDPR has of course changed the game in Europe with regards to being transparent with users, but Gentry feels everyone, regardless of laws, should have this as a best practice.

Now, more than ever, with the increasing amount of data that's being generated in the world, from websites to social media, it's critical to have this level of sensitivity everywhere.

"Data scientists have a responsibility to be unbiased, have integrity, and use their experience to add a positive background to the dataset, rather than let their feelings cloud the model building exercise."

In the near future, Gentry expects to see more regulations like Europe's GDPR to come into action that will dictate how organizations collect and deal with your data. She has a warning for businesses that abuse data – *"people will leave and look for ways to go incognito, which will leave your business with no data at all."*

Conversation with a data scientist

In 2017, Gentry was invited to speak at the Demystifying Data Science conference, hosted by Metis. She gave a talk called *Conversation with a*

Data Scientist. In her talk, she says that *"if you are the type of person that isn't satisfied with an answer and always wants to know more and know why, then data science is the field for you"*. She goes on to say that people shouldn't let the hurdle of learning how to program and other things stop you; you can learn this stuff, and data science is a team effort.

If you just have an understanding of programming, you need to be able to communicate to another person what you need. You can't just take a course and be a data scientist. It takes a long time to understand about linking databases, about how data is structured, etc., *"You can partner up with a programmer, take your ability to uncover insights, and work together as a team"*

What are your thoughts on 'Big Data'?

"Data science has been around for decades, and it's not just big data. I hear a lot of people clumping these two together like they go hand-in-hand, which I agree with to an extent. However, big data needs data science, but data science doesn't necessarily need big data. Most of the data a typical company handles on a daily basis or in-house internally is not big data. Even Facebook and Google break up or segment their data into workable pieces. Data science is big, small, structured, unstructured, messy, clean. It's more than just analytics. As a data scientist, you'll become a liaison between the IT department and the C-suite. What really matters in data science is the team effort and your role as a liaison. You want to be able to give insight, which requires knowledge of your audience."

Steps in the data science process:

It's always helpful to know what steps data scientists take when carrying out a project. These are the standard steps that Gentry follows when starting a data science project:

1. Exploratory: What questions do you want answers to? Such as, "Who are my best customers? Where should I advertise my new product? Where should I place my new product (store and product analysis)?"

2. Gap report: What do you have? vs. What do you need? For example, I may have sales information, but since it's a new product, I need behavioral or demographic data to know what the potential sales numbers might be. Gap analysis forces a company to reflect on what it is and asks what it wants to be in the future.

3. Attaining data you don't have: Open-source, purchase data, build your own data from public sources. Factors include cost, time to receive, loading data, analysis, presentation, and so on. We are collecting more data than ever before, yet many organizations are still looking for better ways to obtain value from their data and compete in the marketplace.

4. Analysis: This isn't something that's done in Excel. You need an experienced staff and the right hardware and software. Complex analysis may run overnight, so make sure you have enough oomph to do it right. You may need to purchase additional equipment or staff.

Social media queen

With over 311,000 tweets as (@data_nerd) and 331,301 followers on LinkedIn to her name, Gentry is also extremely active on social media. Recently, she was mentioned in the list of 'Most Influential Data Scientists' on Twitter and LinkedIn.

"I use all forms of media, since data science is not just a Twitter or Facebook thing. I want everyone to see my comments, from the CEO down to the beginning analyst. I use social media as a way to get the word out about data science and women in technology. I want to make sure the ladies out there know it is possible.

Social media is not as time-consuming as people think. You give good content and you're receptive and you respond to other people and you engage with them."

If you were granted one wish to change something in data science, what would it be?

"I wish data scientists would think more like a CEO; people need to think about business and logic. People focus on programming; don't focus on just the data mining tools, there's no tool that's more important than the other. The preparation of what questions you are trying to answer; don't follow what the data has. Start with the problem, then think about how are you going to solve it. I don't want to influence aspiring data scientists into using a specific tool for their analysis. If you are great at obtaining insights from data, and only know how to use Excel, then you are as much of a data scientist as the others.

Business leaders don't care what tool you use, they care about increasing ROI, save the company money, bring in more customers, etc. The younger generation needs to stop talking so much about programming and start talking about how we can use data to fix business problems. If all you care about is programming, then you should become a programmer, not a data scientist.

Another thing that I feel is important is that college students be exposed to data that isn't pristine. Teach people how to use data that isn't perfect. Colleges need to compensate professors to make it lucrative for experienced people to come and teach. Need to focus on what we do with data and how this will help companies, and how bias will affect data sets."

What are some of your next goals?

"I want to pass off all this knowledge; I want to share my experience and train people, to bring up young data scientists. Then, eventually, get a teaching role in college or some training facility where I can teach people how to do it right. I'm also trying to focus on my family, friends, neighbors, my house, and to have a balanced life."

CRAIG BROWN

SENIOR BIG DATA ARCHITECT & DATA SCIENCE
CONSULTANT

"I like working on the innovative side of data
science and on the technology itself;
rolling up my sleeves and getting messy."

Craig Brown is a leader in the technology industry, but, even more than that, Brown is also a leader in his community. Brown's technical expertise is unquestionable: he has three PhDs, over 25 certifications, and a diverse portfolio of successful projects completed.

"I'm a data scientist, big data architect, and data platform engineer; I get to see the data in all of its aspects. I see the actual information, the platform on which its stored, and the tools that are used to deliver information to the users. I like working on the innovative side of data science and on the technology itself, rolling up my sleeves and getting messy."

Can you talk more about why you chose to complete so many certifications?

"Certifications worked for me as a way to have an edge over other candidates. A good portion of my 30-year career has been spent on consulting. Having a certification helped me add value to my hands-on experience, because experience is limited to what's being asked of you by the client. Certifications became my tradition. They helped me fill in the gaps between what I've done and what I know of the technologies. I'm more proud of my certifications than I am of my 3 PhDs."

Importance of taking risks

On top of this stellar resume, Craig Brown is an individual who advocates for the benefits of taking risks and strives to mentor others so that they can succeed.

Brown's example shows why it can be important to allow young people to participate in activities that come with associated risk. While parents do have a responsibility to protect their children, perhaps Brown can show us how activities that come with risk might make a person stronger and more resilient in the long term. In many ways, our culture has become more risk-averse than any time before. It is becoming less and less socially acceptable for parents to expose children to any risk whatsoever. In an age when allowing children to play unsupervised in the backyard can draw criticism, it can be hard to determine how taking certain risks can actually benefit an individual. To highlight the problem, data shows that the newest generation is half as likely as previous generations to have a license to drive at the age of 16. While driving may indeed be risky, it is also a crucial indicator of independence.

Although he does not like to think that he engaged in risky behavior, Brown is thankful for his early life experience, during which he was able to engage in activities that contained an element of risk. As a result, he experienced consequences that were crucial to his development and later success. Unlike the latest generation, who delays driving their parents' cars as long as possible, Brown chose something riskier as his vehicle of choice. By 16, Brown was wheeling around town on a motorcycle. He found the risk that came with that mode of transportation attractive. Operating a vehicle that was dangerous and fast was exhilarating for the teen.

Brown soon learned that the risk came with consequences, realizing that the adventure of having the motorcycle was balanced against the cost of repairs and the possibility of injury. He credits his motorcycle riding with teaching him a whole myriad of lessons. While others avoided the things they feared, Brown was facing them. He was also able to identify his physical limits. Perhaps most importantly, Brown learned to think through the consequences of his risks. Would he be able to pay for repairs to his bike if he did some damage to it?

For Brown, the life lessons he learned as he worked making pizzas in a deli and riding his motorcycle in his spare time would help him face other decisions as he moved beyond high school. Paradoxically, maybe, parents can learn from this experience: simple jobs, such as pizza making, and experiences like motorcycle riding that come with some risk, can place young people in positions to take control of their lives when they face the challenges that come with adulthood.

Who is your inspiration?

Along with his own life experience, Brown says his father was his biggest inspiration. There is no doubt that boys look up to their fathers, and, in this case, Brown was fortunate to have a strong example. Brown's father modeled a tenacious work ethic. From his prodigious academic record, it is clear that the younger Brown was watching his father closely. Brown also learned the importance of persisting through difficulties.

Brown shares that he watched his father during a time when African American men faced extreme obstacles. In spite of these obstacles, the younger Brown was able to watch his father persevere through personal and professional barriers. Brown's father always set an example of taking the high road. Brown carried these lessons with him as he entered a field that is technically challenging and typically less diverse than other career fields. *"My father pushed me, and when I was a teenager, I didn't understand and wasn't fond of his techniques. Now I can see it for what it was."*

Academic success

"I wasn't an A student in high school, but I was in college. In college, I finally got it. I was also inspired by being a part of an organization: Black Data Processing Associates (BDPA); it was for minorities interested in technology and computer-related fields."

Brown went from making pizzas and riding motorcycles to pursuing academic success and riding motorcycles, and his academic pedigree is superlative. In 1991, Brown completed two bachelor of science degrees. One of the degrees was in computer science and the other was in mechanical engineering. When many people would have been challenged to complete either of the degrees, Brown maintained a 3.8 or higher grade point average in both areas of study.

"I double majored because I took an internship with a phone company in Philadelphia were I was hired as an engineer but was tasked to actually do technology work; I

was a computer programmer and report writer. I enjoyed it and my school advisor told me that it's not engineering, it's computer science, so I double majored."

From those degrees, Brown moved on to earning a Master of Business Administration in 1993. *"I thought an MBA would make me more well-rounded and allow me to better understand the whole picture."* Again, Brown's self-discipline and work ethic shone as he maintained a 3.8 grade point average. While most individuals would have contented themselves with these achievements, Brown did not stop. *"I became a 'professional student' and stayed to get 3 back-to-back PhDs."* Only two years after completing the MBA, Brown earned a Doctor of Philosophy (PhD) in Management Information Systems. In 1998, Brown completed a second PhD in Computer/Information Technology Administration and Management, and, in 2010, Brown completed a third PhD in Computer Engineering. Through his academic journey, his grade point average never fell below 3.8.

Creating your own opportunity

In 1996, long before Brown considered himself a success, he was featured as part of an article about a new breed technical experts. The article, published in the Wall Street Journal, described how a new generation of entrepreneurs with technical backgrounds were abandoning the traditional job model of working for corporations. Brown, prominently featured throughout the article, described his experiences at the age of 29 in this new field. The article speaks to how Brown had to make his own opportunities. It detailed how Brown faced the uncertainty of trying to line up different projects. Unlike the traditional career model, which offered stability, Brown was knee-deep in something new and exciting but far less predictable. He was traveling between continents pursuing different job leads. Each new job presented a new challenge, and Brown found himself constantly pursuing new certifications so that he could face these new challenges with the proper technical skills.

While it was clear that such an adventurous job appealed to Brown's ability to face fears and calculate risks, he was also recently married and expecting his first child. And while the Wall Street Journal article painted an uncertain future for the technical consultant who was abandoning the traditional job model, we now know that the traditional job model, along with the pension and the dinosaur, was going extinct.

Brown credits the article in the Wall Street Journal with making him look differently at himself. Perhaps if others were looking to him to be a leader in the field, he should give himself that much credit as well. The article inspired him to begin examining his own possibilities rather than merely describing his life in terms of what he had accomplished in the past.

Career evolution

Brown describes the evolution of his professional career as beginning with databases. At first, Brown spent most of his energy designing databases. Early on, he admits that he was working on the vessels that held the data and not on the data itself. Eventually, he realized that the technical issues with the databases were not the biggest challenges. The biggest challenges involved ensuring that the data was collected appropriately in the first place. The data quality is even more crucial than the database construction.

Now, Brown brings his highly technical expertise to these data challenges. With his diverse knowledge, he can accurately determine which technology will best apply to the data at issue. Brown's resume, beginning in 1991, reflects his expertise in database technology. Brown has more than twenty years of experiences as a database administrator. Just in this area, he has worked with databases of up to 50,000 users and 50 TB of data.

From his very concrete projects in the 1990s, Brown moved on to larger, more abstract challenges. He began advocating for the use of technology to solve problems for individuals and companies. His technical experience has given him the basis of knowledge he's needed to see what the larger applications of data can do for the private sector. He is a sought-after consultant for both large and small businesses who wish to leverage the power of data for business solutions.

Giving back to the community

Brown wants his legacy to reach even further than his technical contributions to the field of data science. He is very involved in charitable endeavors and community projects. Brown leads by example through his work at EPIC (Empowering, Purpose, Integrity, Character) Youth Sports. This organization seeks to provide a safe but challenging environment for young people. By teaching the fundamentals of basketball and encouraging healthy competition, the organization aims to prepare the next generation of this country to be citizens of character. Brown also works with various other projects that provide disadvantaged children with exposure to potential careers in technical fields. He also advocates for programs that foster healthy lifestyles for young people, as Brown himself enjoys many different sports such as running and golf.

In addition to those admirable projects, Brown has also served as President of the Black Data Processing Associates (BDPA). When Brown first became associated with the organization in the early 1990s, he gained his first exposure to the field of consulting. This organization has worked to enable African Americans and minorities to succeed in the information technology field. Not only does this organization encourage adults, but it has given thousands of high school students the chance to learn crucial technical skills like coding. Leaders like Brown understand that the best way to ensure the success of the next generation of minority data scientists is to give students a hands-on experience early in their lives. Brown credits this organization with helping him attain the level of success that he has enjoyed in his career.

With perhaps the most competitive resume in data science, Brown not only advocates for but also works to achieve a future generation of diverse data scientists that are not just technically proficient but are also leaders of good character. You could not ask for a better combination.

"Since 2009, I got addicted to social media. In my spare time, I mentor young kids, in sports, computer classes, etc. I used social media to let people know what I can help with. This turned into this massive networking activity. I now spend about 10-15 hours a week on social media; I try to gather information and share it; tell people what changes they can start preparing for."

Overcoming difficulties

Brown suffered a serious personal challenge in 2009 when he was diagnosed with pancreatic cancer. Brown faced the illness with the same pluck and determination that he exhibited in the rest of his life. He confesses that motorcycle riding was one way he coped with the diagnosis and treatment. The focus that is required in riding his motorcycle pulled him away from the uncertainties of chemotherapy and the cancer inside of him that kills thousands of people each year. The illness made him reevaluate his lifestyle--he changed what he ate and tried to decrease his stress levels. He also used the experience to try to encourage other cancer patients. A bad diagnosis does not mean that your life is over. He encourages others to safely pursue the hobbies that they enjoyed before their diagnoses.

Writing *Your Untapped Potential*

Brown's personal journey has inspired him to write his book, *Your Untapped Potential: The Supreme Partnership of Self.* While Brown enjoys the technical side of big data, he is also eager to mentor others so that their leadership skills grow alongside their technical skills. In his book, Brown speaks about the importance of not merely looking for a job, but creating one. Just as he realized early in his career that he should look to larger opportunities, he challenges individuals to look beyond simply earning their next paycheck. He likens individuals to software. Just as software goes through multiple versions to correct problems and enhance its functions, individuals should look to see how they can add new skills to their repertoire. He advocates for all people to examine their core competencies and improve those, no matter where they currently find themselves.

Brown states: *"I'm very proud of this book. The book's purpose is to help people move forward and tap into their core competencies. Anyone that reads this book can expect to learn some tricks of the trade to get to the next level. It's not about the position you are in now; it's about elevating yourself. It's about developing your skillset that will add value to companies."*

Proudest accomplishments

When asked about his proudest accomplishments, Brown can name significant projects such as the introduction of cell phone technology by Sprint. Working in that industry at the end of the 1990s was very special, as technology was changing at a rapid pace. Brown is also happy about the diversity that he brings to his career. By possessing a variety of technical skills, Brown has always been able to succeed in every economy.

"I worked at Sprint PCS at the introduction of the cellphone - I was a key member of the team that was involved in the launch in the 1990s. Personally, I'm proud of how I've governed my career. Getting as diverse and relevant with my skillsets has allowed me to be a part of several interesting projects and opportunities."

Speaker, influencer and social media leader

Brown currently bills himself as a senior big data architect and data science consultant. He is an expert in data science. He has multiple other areas of expertise, including machine learning and artificial intelligence. In fact, he regularly participates in panels that discuss topics such as artificial intelligence. In his consulting business, he works to ensure that his clients have the technical solutions that they need.

Brown also works to ensure his clients learn to replicate his solutions to their problems.

He also stays active in the dissemination of information about the growing field of data science through social media. Brown is very conscious of his power to influence the public through his social media contacts. He has a prodigious number of followers on social media, raking in millions of social impressions per day and boasting over 600,000 LinkedIn and 53,000 Twitter followers. He has been ranked second out of the top one hundred big data social influencers.

DJ PATIL

FORMER U.S. CHIEF DATA SCIENTIST

> "A data scientist is that unique blend of skills that can both unlock the insights of data and tell a fantastic story via the data."

When people think about the big players in data, the United States government may not come to mind. However, the United States maintains the largest collection of data in the Northern Hemisphere, if not in the entire world. With all that is contained in the data, including state secrets and the personal information of millions of people, its care and protection has become a crucial issue for the nation.

Enter DJ Patil. In a time when the nation anticipates that the next major world conflict could well be waged with technology, DJ Patil was the first U.S. Chief Data Scientist. *"The reason the Obama appointed me and had me work on things that I did was specifically under the mission: 'to responsibly unleash the power of data to benefit ALL Americans'. In this model it was key to him that I wasn't going to focus on national security items. Rather my focus would be on how to use data to help 'every' American."*

While DJ is now recognized as a leading Data Scientist in his field, his road to influence was not easy. In fact, not many things about his early life indicated that he would achieve such great success later in life. From a young age Patil did not stand out for his academic prowess; however, time after time, he stood up in the face of adversity. This important quality carried him to his place in history as the first U.S. Chief Data Scientist.

Early life

Dhanurjay, now better known as DJ, was born in 1974 to an immigrant family. While his father had traveled from India to study at MIT, Patil would not find his way paved by his father's success. Although Patil was attracted to science, mathematics, and technology, he did not shine in the classroom. He was constantly interested in applying these subjects, but he was much less interested in understanding how the subjects worked. He accumulated quite a resume of pranks. He was able to use his computer skills to hack school grades. He could not tame his tongue enough to suffer through algebra class and ended up getting kicked out and repeating the course during the summer. He even applied his skills to setting off a stink bomb in class, a stunt that got him suspended from school.

Patil credited the same school administrator who suspended him, as he took a chance and invited Patil to participate in a special program with helping less fortunate students from underserved communities buckle down and complete high school. By participating in the program, DJ was able to improve his behavior in class and managed to avoid disciplinary problems at school. This school administrator would later inspire DJ to give a commencement address at Berkeley where he challenged students to take a chance on people.

At which point did you feel most discouraged in life?

"Probably when it was not clear that I was going to graduate from high school. I thought I wasn't going to get in to any college. Luckily, I went to an amazing local community college. And thankfully, my girlfriend at the time was taking calculus; so I took the class with her. That's how I fell in love with calculus."

How did your parents react to your less than stellar academic marks?

"My father knew that I didn't fit in the system. On one hand I think he was just crossing his fingers, hoping for the best; and from another perspective, he was encouraging me to keep doing different things. This gave me freedom; I never felt like I was stupid. I motivated myself to push more. I stopped learning for the grade and was learning because I wanted to."

College acceptance challenges

While Patil did enjoy conducting experiments on high speed photography in a spare room in their house, his academic performance was substandard. High school graduation in 1992 brought Patil to face the truth: he was not accepted into any of the colleges of his choice.

His lack of focus on grades, his pranks, and a low SAT score only garnered him rejections from every college to which he had applied.

Fortunately, Patil's father refused to let his son give up. Although it was a far cry from MIT, DJ started attending De Anza Community College in Cupertino, California, while appealing his rejection from the University of California, San Diego. Part of his motivation to attend the school was the fact that his current girlfriend was also attending, and he signed up for the same classes that she was taking. On his very first day in calculus class, Patil came face to face with his deficient foundation in academics. He understood nothing of the professor's lecture. The professor may well have been speaking a different language.

Where some people may have reacted to the situation by dropping out, Patil chose a different course of action. His next stop was the library. He ravaged the shelves, looking for every high school math text he could find. He was determined to master the fundamentals of the discipline, and he succeeded.

"Once I got my act together in college, I became super boring; I studied on the weekends and took every class I could. I had this deep appreciation of school, because I went to community college with single moms, veterans, and others. Their time in class was a trade off from bringing in money to support their family. They were making a sacrifice to invest in themselves. Their gift to me was to teach me how lucky I was to have opportunity. And I sure as hell wasn't going to waste it."

Continuing his education

Patil's determination paid off, and he was able to transfer to the University of California, San Diego, graduating in 1996 with a degree in Mathematics. *"Oddly enough, I actually graduated a quarter early since I had maxed out on the classes that could be taken. There were a few quarters where I took double the max recommended load of classes."*

Again, he faced challenges with rare determination. While he had been able to make the transition to the four-year institution, he was once again in an unfavorable position. He had not shone academically, and the programs that he wanted to enter did not accept him. Other people would have quit or possibly contented themselves with lesser ambitions.

However, Patil took a chance and sent a personal email to Professor James Yorke at the graduate school (the University of Maryland) that he wanted to attend. This was not just any professor; this was the professor who was widely regarded as the father of the chaos theory (in fact he named the field). Professor Yorke responded with enthusiasm that he should apply through the regular process. Patil's father, a former professor himself, knew that there has to be a special bond between a PhD advisor and student for great science to take place. And he suggested that the two take a road trip and try to have a face-to-face meeting with the Professor. Much to Patil's surprise, Professor Yorke actually went to dinner with the pair. This personal interaction was crucial, as Patil would end up being accepted into the program at the University of Maryland. No other school accepted him. And Professor Yorke would become his advisor.

Patil's work at the University of Maryland was both practical and challenging. Patil, like most students, was strapped for cash and worked as a lecturer to help pay for his studies. On top of working, Patil made meaningful contributions in an area that affects people every day: weather forecasting. Delving into the public data that he could access from the National Oceanic and Atmospheric Administration, Patil analyzed weather patterns. His work was not meant to discover some obtuse theory; rather, it had a practical and positive impact on weather forecasting, enabling more accurate and efficient forecasts to be made. Together with Professor Yorke and other key faculty they pioneered a new approach to using chaos theory to improve weather forecasting.

Post college activities

After completing his PhD, Patil joined the faculty at the University of Maryland. And after the events of September 11, 2001, Patil decided to leverage his talents to help on national security. It was 2004, and the United States was actively engaged in the conflict in Afghanistan and Iraq. Patil led the Threat Anticipation Project for the Department of Defense. This project was trying to harness the power of technology alongside social science to help understand newly emerging threats.

After public service, in 2006, Patil opted to leave the academic world and headed to Silicon Valley. Although he felt ready to take on the problems of the booming tech industry, once again, he was not welcomed with open arms. Just as he had faced rejection after high school and college, none of the big tech companies seemed interested in his skill set. Perhaps his focus on practical problems rather than empty academic success did not fit into the traditional hiring paradigm. *"Part of what I was pitching was that I was deeply interested in this new way to look at data and use it in new ways. That wasn't that interesting for the companies."* The massive influx of people competing for jobs in newly-minted startups made it hard to break into the job market.

Can you share your story about how you got your first job?

"My wife and I were expecting our first kid. I couldn't find any opportunities in NY where she worked so we both decided to pick up and move to the west coast. I interviewed with Google, Yahoo, all these places where I knew people. They said, 'Oh, I don't know what to do with you'. Well, I started thinking, how do I prove my value?

I had a friend who was a consultant at eBay, and they had questions on statistics, so I added value, and I interviewed there. I bombed the interview, because I was asking more questions than I was answering. My mom happened to be at a party, and met the president of Skype at the time. She convinced him to get on a phone with me. He said, 'Oh, you are pretty smart, let's find a role for you' – and that's how I started working for eBay. It was a combination of me adding value and someone taking a shot on me. Then once you're in the role you should always create more than you take. Focus on what you can deliver vs. what's in it for me."

In less than two years at eBay, Patil generated a prodigious eight different patent filings. He began to make a name for himself as an expert in data. He was not interested in data for the sake of data. Rather, he used the information to refine processes, solve problems, and build products people could interact with.

Moving on to LinkedIn

Patil's move to LinkedIn in 2008 was a pivotal move that would open new opportunities for him. Reid Hoffman, the CEO of LinkedIn at that time, understood that the company was facing limitations. They had grown, and millions of people had accounts, but the company was struggling to achieve its vision of connecting people with each other after accounts were created.

Enter Patil. Surrounded by a team of equally motivated data scientists, he looked at individual experiences, identified opportunities where connection could be improved, and then harnessed the power of data to fix the problem. The results of their work were features that are now expected features on the social media site, including Who's Viewed My Profile, Jobs You Might Be Interested In, InMaps, and Skills. As well as a number of key technologies including Kafka, Voldemort, and LinkedIn's A/B testing platform.

How did the term "data scientist" become popular?

"We had no intention on trying to label a field. Facebook and LinkedIn were heading towards their IPOs and the HR departments had issues that there were so many different titles: designers, engineers, analysts, research scientists; they said, 'there only gets to be one title'. Jeff Hammerbacher (who led the Facebook data team) and I were catching up over lunch and talking about how to deal with this;

we went through the list of potential titles: analyst sounded too wall street, research scientist sounded too academic, and different names had other reasons for being rejected. Finally, we agreed on data scientist. The real magic that happened was that LinkedIn team decided to post all the jobs with different titles. We analyzed which jobs people applied to, which titles attracted them. Most people applied to data scientist jobs. We basically 'data scienced' our way into data science.

The reason the term has taken off is because no one knows exactly how to define it. Data scientist is the intersection of all the awesome nerd types. The freedom that the title affords is the secret ingredient.

Back at that the time of LinkedIn we were fighting to prove that us awesome nerds could add disproportionate value. Honestly, we just wanted to make an impact. We wanted to share the message that ridiculously great things can happen if you empower data scientists. People saw that data scientists are changing the trajectory of companies. That gave us runway; as Hillary Mason recently said, 'we won'. Data science doesn't have to be one-dimensional. We can have all these roles and embrace the diversity of the field."

It was around 2008 when Patil began regularly applying the term 'Data Scientist' to what he did, and he began using that title as he hired new employees. By 2012, DJ Patil was pioneering what would become a new field. Alongside Thomas Davenport, Patil published an article in Harvard Business Review. Thomas Davenport is a professor who has published prolifically in the field of business processes. Together, the two wrote "Data Scientist: The Sexiest Job of the 21st Century." While Patil had largely intended the piece to be a recruiting tool for his company, the paper became the battle cry for many organizations that realized how they were ignoring the larger meaning behind the information that they were collecting.

Data artists & artificial intelligence (AI)

"We are just at the beginning of the curve. Right now, AI is phenomenal at repeatable tasks. Most data science is a craft; it's not repeatable. We are in many

ways more like 'data artists'. I'd love for AI to help data scientist clean the data (I still stand by my statement that, unfortunately, 80% of a data scientists' job is cleaning data). Being able to understand nuances and pull insights is a data scientist's job. I'm extremely bullish and not worried at all. AI will help make things scalable. There's ample room for things to evolve. You get to build with data."

The US government

In 2012, while DJ Patil was authoring the paper *Data Scientist: The Sexiest Job of the 21st Century*, the government was actively seeking technology experts to improve the government's services. President Obama filled old jobs and created new jobs for technology experts. By 2015, the Office of Science and Technology Policy, a group created in 1976 to give specialized advice on these topics to the President, determined that a data scientist should join its ranks. Patil was the obvious choice.

DJ Patil became the first U.S. Chief Data Scientist in February of 2015. Patil's mission was simple – to responsibly unleash the power of data to benefit all Americans; but the scope of the work was overwhelming. Patil jumped into the task, releasing a memorandum that outlined his goals. The overarching theme of his goals was to use the government data to bring a concrete benefit to the American public. His hope was to create practices that allowed for sharing of information but at the same time ensured correct management of the data. Additionally, he hoped to be able to recruit other experts to help the government in these endeavors.

Police Data Initiative

These goals would be applied in specific contexts as Patil worked on a series of initiatives. After the shooting of Michael Brown in Ferguson, Missouri, in 2014, President Obama grew concerned about the social implications of the event. The President's Task Force on 21st Century Policing to make recommendations and tasked his team to find new ways to improve policing. As a part of this initiative, several data initiatives leveraged the massive amounts of information that different agencies collected. One of these was the Police Data Initiative. This initiative aimed to begin standardizing data concerning police actions such as stops, searches, and officer-involved shootings. This initiative posited that increased cooperation and flow of information between jurisdictions would improve transparency.

Data-Driven Justice Initiative

Another initiative on policing was the Data-Driven Justice Initiative. This initiative encouraged that safe sharing of data between the criminal justice system and the health care system to help the most vulnerable: those with mental health issues. The key tenet was that instead of putting those with mental health or addiction issues in jail, to redirect them to the appropriate care facility. These programs now cover more than 94 million Americans and are in every major U.S. city and have saved millions of dollars.

Precision Medicine Initiative

Another key area of interest for the first U.S. Data Chief was healthcare and creating collaborations of data. Patil helped to develop the Precision Medicine Initiative (PMI) with the goal of developing a new model for tailored medical treatments. The foundation of this effort would be massive advanced in medical data collection and data science. This project required a unique approach, as Patil had to navigate the competing interests of patient privacy and medical advancement. The PMI was ambitious in that it was designed to develop the largest collection of genetic and medical data set. This information was to be used to help advance cures and treatments for a variety of different conditions that included cancer, rare diseases, and chronic illnesses. While such a database would offer huge advantages to researchers and practitioners, patient information is protected in a variety of ways and must be treated carefully. Along with the PMI, Patil also had to formulate ways to navigate patient privacy in relation to new legislation, the 21st Century Cures Act.

What was the biggest obstacle that you came across in the White House?

"Culture. You see people trying to do amazing things with data and technology. It's silly to assume that data scientists will come in and do all these cool new innovative things. The reason it's silly is you have more than a couple of million employees across the federal government. You don't have to come up with your own ideas. You have to ask the real experts, those that have spent a lifetime serving the public. If you ask around, you'll get so many great ideas. Things like 'can we make this go faster? Or can we make this thing bigger' – that's really what we did. It was scout and scale. Scout for ideas and see how you can scale.

Of course, culture was not uniform; it was all over the place. We spoke about making data more accessible by using the latest technologies that facilitate storage and download of large data sets. And some people in the government weren't excited about those ideas. They highlighted real issues, and once those issues were addressed and suddenly data started to be used in this remarkable way.

There are also people that just don't want change. The Department of Defense is trying to move to the cloud, and traditional companies who have been making millions on contracts using outdated technology say 'oh no, you won't', because it threatens their model of business."

Importance of diversity

"When you are in public service, it is so important that the team around you represents the constituents. The morning staff meeting at the White House was held in the Roosevelt room, right outside the Oval Office; when you look around the room, it looks like America; people from all walks of life. It helps to represent America's perspectives. The people around the table need to appreciate the complexity of data and understand its impact. This allows us to make better decisions."

After the White House

DJ Patil's work in the White House came to an end with President Obama's leaving office. Some of the accomplishments from his time in the White House include more than 40 Chief Data Officers being hired, over 90 million Americans covered by the healthcare reforms, Cancer moonshot research is underway, and Precision Medicine Initiative (PMI) has launched and the first studies are coming in.

"The work that I've done with the government will see most of its results and impact in the future; that's still ahead of us".

While Patil was not able to see the fruition of some of his work, he counseled others to continue to collaborate with data scientists. Although he is no longer in the White House, Patil continues to do what he does best. He continues to tenaciously advocate for data science. He does this out of a desire to harness the power of data to make concrete differences in the lives of people.

"People may think that since there isn't currently a Chief Data Scientist in the White House that progress has stopped, and the truth is far from it. When we left the administration, there were more than 40 chief data scientists and data officers. Recently, the Marine Corp had a call out there to hire a Chief Data Officer. The National Institutes for Health (NIH) is looking for a data strategist to figure out how to use data even more. As data people, we are winning. We've proven that having a data scientist has an impact. I truly hope that the first Chief Data Scientist of the Marine Corp will be a woman, because I can't think of anyone better suited to provide a unique perspective to a field that has been traditionally biased to the male gender."

Which of your roles do you think had a large impact on society?

"My work in academia; in weather forecasting specifically. I focused on something we all experience: the weather. We now think of the weather as these little icons we get on the phone, we see a sun icon and we know it'll be warm that day; we see

a lightning bolt going through a cloud icon and we know to bring an umbrella with us. Behind these little icons sits petabytes of data. Some of the most sophisticated models that were ever created. This is an extraordinary problem that impacts peoples' lives; predicting storms, floods, etc.

My interest in weather data started when I was searching for a thought-provoking data set to play around with. I came across weather data with over 50 years' worth of weather forecasts in 4-hour increments, of real observations. I would download data and look for patterns. There was so much data that I realized I needed more computers. Luckily, I was able to take over all the department's computers at night, doing a lot of ETL (extract, transform, load), trying to clean the data and look for patterns. I would go to the meteorology department with findings. Sometimes I would actually find something interesting. This allowed us to realize that we can characterize the complexities and then we verify them."

The technique that DJ and his colleagues developed is called the Maryland Ensemble Kalman Filter for atmospheric data assimilation. That technology is now being implemented in every weather forecasting system.

What are you working on now?

"Trying to figure out how we continue to change the curve on healthcare. Creating truly tailored medical programs for people; precision medicine. Collecting data from a million volunteers to find new ways to think about disease. What would it look like if we treated everyone in the healthcare system like our own family? I think we can really do that. We are building a new plan that will try to do that in a very novel way. I get to partner with some of my previous colleagues to try and take on that mission.

I'm also trying to figure out how to push the dialogue of data ethics. How do we do more? It's an idea of an oath. What would a great checklist look like for a data scientist before we launch products? Ethics should be part of conversations in interviews, in colleges, in high schools. This would drastically change the game.

I'm working with other colleagues to write our perspectives and learnings on how we addressed issues and how they can solve problems with data in their own way."

What was the hardest thing you ever had to do?

"At LinkedIn, we had a reduction in force, a layoff, after the financial collapse. I had to lay off people. These were great people; I didn't feel good about it. It was agonizing. I never had done this before, and I wanted to make sure people landed on their feet. I decided that I would work hard to make sure these people were okay. From my team, we had to lay off 2 people, but they were very valuable. These people have gone on to do other great things, and we've stayed in touch."

What would you tell your kids when they are teenagers, if you feel they aren't fitting into the system?

Patil has 2 kids, a boy and a girl, ages 9 and 11. *"They teach you so much, and have made me a better person. I would tell them that they are in control of their destiny more than they think they are. Figure out what system will work out for you. I don't have to figure it out for you. I wish I had told this to myself. I see people complain that they can't get an internship for the summer; my view is go create your own. You can take the massive open online courses or 'MOOCs', go to every hackathon that you can, construct your own education. There are communities now. If I had come across these data science communities early on, it would be so empowering. I'd say find your own tribe. No one else can find your tribe except you; focus all your energy on this."*

DREW CONWAY

FOUNDER AND CEO AT ALLUVIUM

"If your job is to help your business or customers make better decisions using data, then I'd say you're a data scientist."

D rew Conway is a data scientist well-known for his Venn-diagram definition of data science as well as for applying data science to study terrorism. Conway is the leading expert in the application of computational methods to social and behavioral problems at large scale. He has advised and consulted companies across many industries, ranging from start-ups to Fortune 100 companies, as well as several academic institutions and government agencies. He started his career in counter-terrorism as a computational social scientist in the U.S. intelligence community.

Conway is the Founder and CEO of Alluvium, a company focused on putting machine intelligence at the frontline of businesses in the foundational industries of the global economy. Alluvium's products enable these businesses to leverage all of their complex data streams and provide real-time decisions and operational support.

Which term applies to you: data scientist, statistician, computer scientist, or something else?

"Technically, my undergraduate degree is in computer science, so that term can be applied. I was actually double-major in computer science and political science, however, so it wouldn't tell the whole story. I have always been most interested in answering social science problems with the tools of computer science, math and statistics.

I have struggled a bit with the term 'data scientist.' About 10 years ago, when it seemed to be gaining a lot of popularity, I bristled at it. Like many others, I complained that it was simply a corporate rebranding of other skills, and that the term 'science' was appended to give some veil of legitimacy. Since then, I have warmed to the term, but—-as is often the case—-only when I can define what data science is in my own terms. Now, I do think of what I do as being data science, that is, the blending of technical skills and tools from computer science, with the methodological training of math and statistics, and my own substantive interest in questions about collective action and political ideology.

I think the term is very loaded, however, and when many people invoke it they often do so as a catch-all for talking about working with a certain a set of tools: R, map-reduce, data visualization, etc. I think this actually hurts the discipline a great deal, because if it is meant to actually be a science, the majority of our focus should be on questions, not tools."

Education

Conway received his BA from Hamilton College (New York) in 2004, where he double-majored in Computer Science and Political Science. He was awarded a MacCracken fellowship and earned his Ph.D. in Political Science from New York University in May 2013. His research focused on computational methods for political science.

Between his studies, he worked in Washington, DC in the defense and intelligence communities for four years. As 'an all-source analyst', his specific role was to apply statistical and computational methods to problems of social dynamics and organizations of interest for the Department of Defense/Intelligence Community.

How did you get started in data?

"I got started before data science was a discipline. I started my career in the US intelligence community. My title was a Social Scientist; I worked across several different problem areas. I can describe my background in two buckets — a) basic research, almost academic in nature, and b) traditional intelligence work. I spent time thinking about how to support deployed war fighters. My focus was around military intelligence, so my customers were the men and women that were serving in the field.

I had to work on answering difficult questions — if a field commander wants to do a patrol in a certain neighborhood, when is the safest time to do it? I was very fortunate that I was able to both learn in an environment surrounded by talented people and also have challenging problems to think about.

The team was around 20 people, but we worked in small teams focused on different roles and responsibilities. Questions that we were answering were coming from the field; it was more of a tactical support function. There was all this data, and we had to answer questions from this data. The questions asked were often specific but open-ended. Questions about people, materials, or money moving around; they would want to know exactly where it was. We had visceral feedback loops from our manager in terms of the quality and direction of our work, so if we were going down the wrong path, we were able to quickly fix it."

When asked about what the biggest challenge he faced while working in the military intelligence group, Conway states: *"The quality of our data and the frequency of data collection presented challenges. Turnaround time was a challenge, but the work is a function of that."*

The Data Science Venn Diagram is born

In September of 2010, Conway joined a group of the most sophisticated thinkers on all things data for a half-day session in NYC to help O'Reily organize their upcoming Strata conference. One of the break-out sessions was focused on issues related to teaching data science, which inevitably led to a discussion on the skills needed to be a fully competent data scientist.

"I had the benefit of talking to smart people on a regular basis. The Venn Diagram is a symbol or representation of a lot of different ideas put together that attempt to define data science as an interdisciplinary pursuit. It was also an attempt to define what it's not. At that time, there was some resistance to data science, people saying that this was just a statistics role and the people are trying to exploit the job market."

The Venn Diagram was first published on a community blog called Dataists.com.

How to read the Data Science Venn Diagram

The primary colors of data: hacking skills, math and statistics knowledge, and substantive expertise. In order to be in this market, you need to speak <u>hacker.</u> Being able to manipulate text files at the command-line, understanding vectorized operations, thinking algorithmically; these are the hacking skills that make for a successful data hacker.

Once you have acquired and cleaned the data, the next step is to actually extract insight from it. In order to do this, you need to apply appropriate <u>math and statistics methods,</u> which requires at least a baseline familiarity with these tools.

In the third critical piece— <u>substance</u>—data plus math and statistics only equates to machine learning, which is great if that is what you are interested in, but not if you are doing data science.

Science is about discovery and building knowledge, which requires some motivating questions about the world and hypotheses that can be brought to data and tested with statistical methods.

On the flip-side, substantive expertise plus math and statistics knowledge is where most traditional researchers fall. Doctoral level researchers spend most of their time acquiring expertise in these areas, but very little time learning about technology. Part of this is the culture of academia, which does not reward researchers for understanding technology.

Finally, a word on the hacking skills plus substantive expertise danger zone. This is where Conway places people who, 'know enough to be dangerous', and is the most problematic area of the diagram. In this area, people are perfectly capable of extracting and structuring data, likely related to a field they know quite a bit about, and probably even know enough R to run a linear regression and report the coefficients, but they lack any understanding of what those coefficients mean. It is from this part of the diagram that the phrase 'lies, damned lies, and statistics' emanates, because either through ignorance or malice this overlap of skills gives people the ability to create what appears to be a legitimate analysis without any understanding of how they got there or what they have created.

Eight years have passed since this Venn Diagram was illustrated, is there a need to update it?

"There's no need to update it. It continues to be useful, especially to those new to the discipline. One thing I think is cool is when I see people putting this diagram up on the presentations at conferences as a way to describe the role of a data scientist. I think it's a useful image to introduce what data science is and what it's not."

The struggle in defining these skills is that it is unclear how to distinguish among hackers, statisticians, subject matter experts, their intersections, and where data science fits. It was in an attempt to simplify the discussion around the skills needed to be a data scientist, that Conway developed the Data Science Venn Diagram.

What was your involvement in starting up DataKind

Conway is also the co-founder of DataKind and currently a member of their advisory board. DataKind harnesses the power of data science in the service of humanity. The vision of DataKind states: 'We are meticulously focused on bringing data science in all its forms to those who share our vision of a sustainable planet in which we all have access to our basic human needs. We envision a world where organizations tackling those problems have the same access to data science resources that Wall St. and Silicon Valley have.'

"There's an active data community in NYC with several passionate people. Jake Porway (another DataKind Co-Founder) is one of those people. We met

at Columbia University and discussing the fact that there are all these skilled individuals that are working on 'small problems' that would likely want to help other people solve more meaningful problems. It occurred to us that there are also several social organizations that have a bunch of data that they collect. We decided to try and get these two groups of individuals together.

We started in NYC and saw the amazing outcome; we then went to the west coast and saw the same level of excitement. We decided that this was a great opportunity to expand the operation. Since I've been involved in startups before, I was able to help out with funding and the legal side of the operations. The organization now is very successful."

DataKind launched in 2011 and are headquartered in New York City and have Chapters in the UK, Bangalore, Dublin, San Francisco, Singapore, and Washington DC.

"I've stayed on the Advisory Board. I'm there to answer questions and provide support; I'm really proud of the work that Jake has done with this group."

Project Florida

In February 2014, Conway announced that he was excited join Project Florida as their Head of Data. Project Florida is an NYC-based hardware/software startup working to harness an expansive breadth of data to improve health outcomes for individuals and help people better understand their health. His role was to lead and nurture a team of world-class data scientists and engineers to build parts of the core product.

His main reason for being excited to join Project Florida was because it would allow him to improve health outcomes and empower people to lead healthier lives. As Head of Data, he was in charge of running the team responsible for developing and delivering these results.

Conway later went on to start his own company, Alluvium.

Why did you start Alluvium and what's the vision?

"It was the next chapter in my career; I wanted to help push data science into areas where they were not fully formed. Specifically, to support the men and women that need to make decisions and are facing constraints. My early career was in support of this broader vision. Alluvium was born out of a specific technical vision as well as the opportunity to take part in this transformation.

The birth of my second child came around the same time that Project Florida, a startup I was heavily involved in, went under and lost its funding earlier in the year. In thinking about what to do next, I was motivated to start Alluvium as a company that could enhance human decision-making as a function of the increase in data generated in the physical world. The biggest opportunity for a product in this space is in the large industrial spaces that are already generating a ton of data but are underserved by the software incumbents that exist there."

What type of work are you doing at Alluvium?

Alluvium aims to conquer one of big data's greatest unsolved challenges for complex industrial operations with expert human operators. It has unique technology that extracts data from all elements of complex industrial operations - tablets, sensors, as well as industry-specific assets - with no expectations of compute resources or network bandwidth. This breakthrough allows machine learning processing to occur at the edge of systems where human operators need data most – in real-time.

"We are building human operator-centered analytic tools for what is being called the 'Industrial Internet of Things.' The motivation at Alluvium is to build in various parts of different industries many products that perform inference, or make choices, to enhance the user experience based on data. Our engineers and data scientists are thinking about how to solve problems that will arise over the course of the next decade or more as new types of instrumentation arise and data availability improves."

Alluvium uses Mesh Intelligence; could you talk more about it?

"Mesh Intelligence is a term that our team created to describe the underlying technologies used. It frees the data from proprietary systems, transforms it into rich information streams, and provides real-time insights to human operators for immediate action."

What are you focused on in the near future?

"This year, we are focused on getting our core product to as many customers as we can. We are a relatively young company, therefore; we are also working on improving performance and user experience."

Machine Learning for Hackers and *Machine Learning for Email*

In addition to leading a business, Conway is the co-author of *Machine Learning for Hackers: Case Studies and Algorithms to Get You Started,* which is targeted towards experienced programmers interested in crunching data and looking to get started with machine learning. He provides a series of hands-on case studies, instead of a traditional math-heavy presentation, to allow readers to understand machine learning and statistics tools.

He is also co-author of *Machine Learning for Email: Spam Filtering and Priority Inbox.* This is a succinct guide that is focused on showing readers how to use machine learning to work with email. This book also includes a short tutorial on using the popular R language to manipulate and analyze data.

What inspired you to write *Machine Learning for Hackers*? Who was your target audience?

"In 2011, John Myles White (my co-author) and I were having a lot of conversations with other members of the data community in New York City about

what a data science curriculum would look like. During these conversations, people would always cite the classic texts: Elements of Statistical Learning, Pattern Recognition and Machine Learning, etc., which are excellent and deep treatments of the foundational theories of machine learning. From these conversations, it occurred to us that there was not a good text on machine learning for people who thought more algorithmically. That is, there was not a text for 'hackers', people who enjoy learning about computation by opening up black boxes and getting their hands dirty with code.

It was from this idea that the book, and eventually the title, were born. We think the audience for the book is anyone who wants to get a relatively broad introduction to some of the basic tools of machine learning and do so through code—-not math. This can be someone working at a company with data that wants to add some of these tools to their belt, or it can be an undergraduate in a computer science or statistics program that can relate to the material more easily through this presentation than the more theoretically heavy texts they're probably already reading for class.

If you were granted one wish to change something about the data science space, what would that wish be?

"In the data science profession, I'd love to change the culture around recruiting and interviewing. I tend to partly blame myself, with the creation of the Venn Diagram, for the culture that exists today. People are looking for the unicorns and ninjas in data science interviews. Companies try to push out people that don't have all 3 aspects of the role, and it creates a negative pattern to filter out skilled candidates just because they aren't able to define some trivial concept. I think the culture is changing for good, because the role is being broken up into specializations. If your job is to help your business or customers make better decisions using data, then I'd say you're a data scientist."

What is your advice for someone to wants to go into data science?

"The most successful data scientists I know are those driven by a curiosity for solving problems through data. To that end, I recommend starting by thinking

about what kinds of problems they find most interesting. From there, go out and try to find some data in the problem area and begin experimenting. Run some basic summary statistics on the data, plot some basic graphs, or even build a simple model. This is also a great way to learn the relevant tools and methods, the result of which can become a nice asset in a person's portfolio. This also, typically, leads people to ask a lot of new questions, which creates a virtuous feedback loop of learning and community discovery."

What are your next big projects?

"Running the startup is my main focus and is more than a full-time job. I also have two young kids (3 years old and 5 years old), so I hope to spend a lot of time with them."

KIRK BORNE

PRINCIPAL DATA SCIENTIST AND EXECUTIVE ADVISOR AT BOOZ ALLEN HAMILTON

"Humans are born data scientists; we are born curious, we ask a lot of questions, and we are good at detecting patterns."

K irk Borne enjoys finding solutions through data. He loves to explore data, make new discoveries, develop a hypothesis to explain these discoveries, and then test those hypotheses. As the Principal Data Scientist at Booz Allen Hamilton, he is able to exercise his Data Scientist role across numerous internal and external projects: human resources, organizational change, training and mentoring, marketing, customer engagement, behavior analytics, risk mitigation, novelty discovery, thought leadership, socialization of data science across organizations and industries, data technologies, predictive and prescriptive analytics, and geospatial-temporal modeling, among many others. He works with clients in the federal sector, within numerous commercial industries, and with nonprofit organizations

How did you get started in data?

"I guess you could say I started my career in the stars. My education was in physics and astronomy. Then I was doing astrophysics, and it always involved data analysis and data collection. But my 'day job' actually was supporting NASA contracts, including the NASA Hubble Space Telescope. I also did work at the National Space Science Data Center. It all included data systems and large data sets; I was always surrounded by data. In the late '90s, some of the data sets were going off the charts in terms of size. I realized something was dramatically changing, and I started looking into data mining and machine learning algorithms, to help scientists explore the data. It became a mix of what we call data management and data analytics."

Skipping lunch in high school

In the 1970s, when Borne was in high school, he found out that some of his math classmates were skipping lunch. Apparently, they found a small office next to the math classroom and were learning to program computers. They were learning the FORTRAN language; once Borne witnessed this, he was in awe and had been hooked. It wasn't long before he joined them and got involved with implementing several math formulas, generating various math tables, and solving homework assignments. In college and grad school, Borne went into astrophysics.

Why astrophysics?

"Caltech was (and still is) the world's leading university for astronomy and astrophysics graduate education. Ever since high school, my goal was to go to Caltech and use the big telescopes at Mount Palomar Observatory, whose astronomical images appeared in all of the astronomy books that I read during my youth. In order to pursue a career in astronomical research, a PhD is required, and Caltech is second-to-none for that."

Afterwards, he continued his astronomical data analysis and computational astrophysics research projects in various postdoctoral positions. He worked as an instructor at the University of Michigan; at the time of the personal computer (PC) revolution; and was lucky enough to be able to use a discount purchase opportunity (offered to university staff members) to buy a home PC. He started using that PC to write some simple programs to work with other kinds of data, such as his family finances.

Family & kids

After Michigan, he and his wife moved to Washington DC, where he received a Carnegie Fellowship within the Carnegie Institution of Washington. Not long after, Borne had become a father to twin girls.

"We adopted the twins (when they were 9 weeks old); we didn't have 9 months to prepare, we had about a week. We registered at an adoption agency, did the home study, had the investigations, etc. In those days, it was a rare occasion for children to be available. The typical wait time was 5 years; the home study itself takes 5-6 months. My wife had just started a job in the federal government working with the Navy.

We had no anticipation for anything happening for several years from that point. But, 10 days later, on a Wednesday evening, we received a phone call from the agency and they said 'we have twins for you.' They needed a younger couple to handle two babies at once, and my wife and I were exactly the folks that they were seeking. The Wednesday after that, we were there picking up the twins. We went from zero preparation to being parents of two kids. My wife and I both had a flu bug, I had no energy or enthusiasm on the phone call and they actually asked if we were sure we wanted to do this; which we absolutely did want. We had an army of friends that showed up at our apartment with baby clothes, cribs, etc.

Once my kids where older, I remember creating little computer games on my PC for my children. My twin daughters now have kids of their own – I have 3 grandchildren."

The Hubble Space Telescope Science Institute

In 1985, Borne's unique skills caught the attention of the Hubble Space Telescope Science Institute in Baltimore, Maryland. Borne's name was mentioned by his mentor at Carnegie and he went in for an interview and was hired on the spot.

It was a cold morning on Jan. 28, 1986, when the space shuttle *Challenger* was supposed to fly into space. Temperatures dipped below freezing. There were certain people at NASA and among contractors that worried about the integrity of the seals on the solid rocket boosters in cold weather. The *Challenger* launched at 11:38 a.m. Eastern time in front of heavy media attention. Tragedy struck as the Challenger broke up 73 seconds after launch in front of the television cameras. 'Flight controllers here are looking very carefully at the situation. Obviously, a major malfunction', the NASA launch commentator said as pieces of the shuttle fell from the sky into the Atlantic, leaving all seven astronauts dead. NASA made technical changes to the shuttle and the program resumed flights in 1988.

Borne reflects on the day of the incident. *"The day of the Challenger launch, it was still a novelty to see the shuttle go into space. It was widely broadcast. I was in my office working, several people I worked with were in the auditorium watching the live feed, and then the shuttle blew up and people were killed. People in the auditorium were stunned and spent the next 6 hours just there watching the replays over and over again, listening to discussions of what could've happened. They sat together suffering through the tragedy. I was in my office working; we didn't have social media, so no one bothered to think to notify others in the office of this tragedy. Plus, I was the new person. So, when I came out of my office at 5pm that evening, several hours after the tragedy, I remember being shocked when I was told of the terrible news."*

After the Challenger tragedy, all shuttle flights were put on hold for several years, including the planned launch of the Hubble Space Telescope. That delay gave people some extra time to evaluate the readiness of the various Hubble systems. One of the systems that needed a total overhaul was the scientific proposal processing system, and they needed someone with a fresh perspective as well as strong skillsets to do the job. Borne was asked to take the lead. He learned and spent the next few years designing, code-writing, integrating, testing, deploying, and managing the entire system! In 1990, the Hubble Telescope scientific proposal entry, processing, and reporting system worked perfectly, and Borne received a major award in 1991 for his great efforts.

Career progression

Borne was later promoted to NASA Project Scientist for the Hubble Science Data Archive, tasked with bringing the new data system online and validating its use for scientific data access, exploration, and discovery. His group received another major award in 1994 after successful completion of that project.

He presented later that year on the comprehensive science data verification plans and the database system. This presentation led to a conversation with a NASA senior manager seeking a contractor employee manager for the Astrophysics Data Facility (ADF) within

NASA's Space Science Data Operations Office at the Goddard Space Flight Center in Greenbelt Maryland. In 1995, Borne was hired.

His responsibility was to oversee the acquisition, ingest, management, and public dissemination of the scientific data sets from all of NASA's thousands of astronomy and space science experiments since the start of NASA.

A few years after, he began learning about data mining. Though he wasn't yet an expert, he quickly learned who the experts were. Borne created a website *NASA's Data Mining Resources for Space Science*, which was a long, curated list of cool data mining resources that he found on the Internet: algorithms, methods, software packages, tutorials, research papers, white papers, popular articles, lectures, conferences, expert interviews, and more. He didn't know the reach and influence of the website until October 2001, when his office phone rang – the unknown voice at the other end of the line asked him, 'Can you brief the President tomorrow morning on data mining?' After recovering from his initial shock, he said 'Do you mean THE President?' and they did in fact mean the President! Borne didn't end up briefing the President at that time but it was a real eye-opener!

Shutting down the ADF

Several months passed and we learned that NASA had plans to shut down the ADF. One of the members of the advisory committee meetings was the Dean of the School of Computational Sciences at George Mason University. He told Borne that he liked what he was doing and wanted to offer him a faculty position in his program. Borne then told him a secret - he wanted to create the first Data Science undergraduate degree program to teach data science and promote data literacy skills to the next generation workforce. In 2003, Borne joined GMU and established that B.Sc. program a few years later.

Why did you want to start this program? Why is it important to promote data literacy skills?

"For me, data literacy is on the same par as other literacies we promote in our education system, like reading, writing, and arithmetic. Literacy also includes an understanding of history and cultures; literacy makes you a well-rounded person, because you can carry on a conversation, you can understand the world you live in, and you can be a productive worker in that world.

Since everything is now digital and everything is producing data – our social media, our cars, our refrigerators – the businesses of the world that will make the biggest splashes and the biggest revenues are those that will make the best use of those data streams and digital signals. And they're looking for people that know how to do it. We need to not just train people in skills – as far as machine learning skills go, very few will actually learn those. But every person needs to learn what data is. And it's not just all the positive issues. There are other issues around data privacy and ethics – having an understanding of both the positives and the negatives, including what could go wrong. We have to work to learn the limitations of data.

There was once a politician who said he was shocked to see that half of the students in the United States were below average. When people are surprised at this statement, it illustrates why we need data literacy skills. By definition, the average lies directly in the middle of a set of numbers (assuming normal or symmetric distribution). Therefore, 50% of scores will be above and 50% will be below at any given time.

Thoughts on formal college education

"I think a college education must prepare people in terms of thinking skills, critical thinking, problem solving, etc. College education value doesn't derive just from the content; it must also train people to collaborate, communicate, to reason, to learn the soft skills of data science. College education is still necessary, though the content delivered in college can't last you a lifetime anymore. Lifelong learning is important; you have to exercise that part of your brain and college is a good place to do that. Success metrics shouldn't be limited to how well you do on an exam.

When I taught the Introduction to Data Science course at the university, several of the students that took my class expressed their fears of math and science. I made it clear to students that whatever math they needed to learn, I would teach it to them in class. I actually taught them calculus but didn't tell them it was calculus until they learned it. Then they were surprised that they were able to learn calculus.

Learning how to learn is important; in the modern age, with technology changing so rapidly, you have to continuously keep learning."

We are born data scientists

"Humans are born data scientists; we are born curious, we ask a lot of questions, and we are good at detecting patterns. When children play, they sort their toys by color, shape, function. They know they can build a castle with blocks but not balls and they know you can play soccer with a ball but not blocks. These are things data scientists do, classification, sorting, indexing, etc.

We need to start by teaching the teachers, then they will go and teach the students every year. Also, training programs for guidance counselors would be helpful."

Social media popularity

In 2012, the U.S. President announced the National Big Data Initiative; 'By improving our ability to extract knowledge and insights from large and complex collections of digital data, the initiative promises to help accelerate the pace of discovery in science and engineering, strengthen our national security, and transform teaching and learning.'

As a result, interest in data science exploded. At this time, Borne had a Twitter account and posted regularly to have his personal log of all things data, as well as to inform his followers. One day, a friend of his, Carla Gentry, asked him, 'How does it feel to be the #2 big data influencer on Twitter in the world?' His response was, 'WHAT?!?' This is when he realized that what he was doing really resonated with several other data science enthusiasts.

This popularity resulted in a large increase in job opportunities; Borne received at least two requests per week since 2013 – none of which were lucrative enough to tempt him to leave his dream job as a tenured full professor promoting data literacy skills to the next generation workforce; until recently.

Making the move to Booz Allen Hamilton

A few years later, Borne became aware of an established corporation, not far from his home that piqued his attention. It was Booz Allen Hamilton – where Borne is currently working as their Principal Data Scientist (as of May 2015). He admired the company for several reasons, including that they now employ several hundred data scientists. They have established a world-class, data-driven business culture; they wrote a fabulous and freely available *Field Guide to Data Science*, and they are passionately dedicated to 'Teaching data science and promoting data literacy skills to the next generation workforce.'

Many people don't leave academia after they get tenure, what has the change been like?

"Several of my colleagues in the academic world thought I was kind of nuts to become a management consultant. So, I'd say, 'Well, it's not really any different than what I've always done.' It's three words to me, 'data to action.' Data to action is what we always did in our science. We collect data, then we decide what to do. We write our research paper, we do another experiment, or we find some new colleagues to help us understand it, or we write a new proposal. It looks different, but it's not really all that different.

Now that I get to do all this cool data science stuff across many, many different industries, different organizations, different sectors — healthcare, cybersecurity, national defense — I get to have conversations about the power of data in a lot of different places."

What excites you most about recent developments and the future of data science?

"The opportunity to work with many different businesses and disciplines is truly the most exciting aspect of the work. Data scientists can work in many areas – for example, I work with people in astrophysics, aerospace engineering, transportation safety, banking, finance, retail, medical research, text analytics, climate modeling, remote sensing, and more. I now call myself a trans-disciplinary data scientist because my work in data science transcends discipline boundaries – I do not need to become an expert in those fields (i.e., not multidisciplinary) in order to work with people with a different domain of expertise than mine. I see a very bright future as more and more organizations get on board the big data / data science train – there are many new technologies, algorithms, problems to solve, and things to do. It is almost overwhelming, but it is definitely exhilarating. My favorite catch phrase these days is 'Never a dull moment!' That sums it all up."

Any words of wisdom for Big Data / Data Science students or practitioners starting out?

"Start early and often in doing, in learning, and in absorbing data science. It takes some serious education and training, but it is worth it. Be true to yourself – know your aptitudes, your skills, your interests – don't force something that isn't there. There is a place for everyone in this data-rich world. Don't underestimate the power of curiosity, communication, and collaboration skills. They will take you further than just about anything else in life. Above all else, be enthusiastic and passionate about it. If you can see the power, discovery potential, and wonder of big data, then the passion and enthusiasm will follow. The future is very bright for those who are able to derive insights from big data, in any discipline or any job. Find the right opportunity and pursue it. There will never be a dull moment after that."

MICO YUK

CO-FOUNDER OF BI BRAINZ GROUP | AUTHOR, DATA VISUALIZATION FOR DUMMIES | CREATOR, BI DASHBOARD FORMULA METHODOLOGY | CREATOR, DATA NATION PODCAST

"People want artificial intelligence, but they also want control. Having both is difficult."

If you had to describe Mico Yuk in one word, 'energy' might be a prime contender. In a field associated with introverts and academics who might prefer silence over speaking, Yuk's passionate media presence is distinct from others in the data field. 'Unique' could be another word to describe her. In what is typically a less diverse field, she provides strong female leadership and a vibrant Caribbean heritage. Whether it is a social media post (LinkedIn, Twitter, Facebook), a YouTube video, a blog post, or a podcast, Mico Yuk brings practical advice and passion with a focus on data storytelling and other key components that can drive success for businesses.

Yuk passionately pursued her interests from a young age. By age 12, Yuk knew that she was into technology and building architecture. Although she did not realize it, she would later be able to mix her love for art with technology to create a winning formula.

How did you get started in data? What is driving your passion?

"I wanted to match my artistic side with my interest in computers. When I first learned about a thing called data visualization, I was hooked! I was fascinated that I could take all my data, condense it into a single visualization, then have people use it to make big decisions. There's so much power in the ability to visualize data."

Yuk completed high school early, at the age of 15. She considered attending art school, but her parents, concerned about her lack of future income, steered her in a different direction. She attended the University of Miami and graduated in 2004 with a degree in computer engineering and a minor in mathematics— a far cry from art school.

It seems that your parents influenced your choice of major. Did they make the right decision?

"In addition to my mom, I got advice from my counselors and a few very well to do business people on my island. In the end, even though I loved art, I loved my then new Compaq desktop computer sitting in my room more. I was already playing around with web design (not much to see online in 1995), so I figured I would go the

coding and design route. I left for college with the goal of working on computers and somehow incorporating my art skills. I originally signed up to be an architectural engineer but within a few weeks switched over to computer engineering. I have zero regrets. Engineering taught me how to think through any problem logically, and that has led to a great part of my success."

What do you think other parents should do when facing a child that has some interest in a less practical degree?

"Exploration is key. My parents exposed us to so many different things, in retrospect I realize how blessed we were. Starting from middle school where I performed in 'The Tempest' play as a part of our drama class. I played the flute and performed at multiple large events on my island. I competed in our 6th-grade science fair with a marijuana fish poisoning detection system and won 2nd place. At age 12, I begged for my first computer the minute AOL dial-up became available in our home, which is how I started programming in HTML. In 9th grade, I woke up at 4 am and played tennis with my biology teacher each day before class. I could keep going, but the point is: Exposure is key! I think the more exposure, the better and more well-rounded your child will be.

However, the decision should reside with your child. The worst thing for anyone to face is doing four years of college for someone else. It's too important of a life decision. Parents, give your opinions, but then respect your child's decision.

If you are really opposed to your child's choice, seek out someone who is in the field who is successful and ask them: 1) to have lunch with your child to discuss how the profession works and what to expect, 2) if your child can work for free after school for a month to get a feel for the industry. Then let your child decide on their degree. All professions have three levels, the top, the middle and the bottom performers. If someone loves what they do, they are going to be at the top, that's all that matters. Mediocrity is like cancer to our souls. Best to avoid at all costs."

Early career

Out of college, Yuk took a job as a Senior Research Analyst at her Alma Mater University of Miami creating algorithms to calculate the schools' athletic, average GPA using SaS mainframe and reporting the scores to Forbes. Although the term data scientist didn't exist back then, Yuk was doing the sorts of tasks that would later become associated with the new career field. From this role, she began to look for other opportunities. When she was hired to design and build supply chain dashboards for Ryder Logistics, she found her niche. Dashboards are visual representations of data. It allows decision-makers to visualize their key performance indicators (KPIs) and quickly understand whether or not the company is healthy. When properly designed, dashboards provide real-time data that can be used in a variety of ways. Yuk had finally found the intersection of art and data!

What were some of the barriers that you encountered as you left college and entered the job market?

"I took 6 and 1/2 years to graduate from undergrad after dropping out of college twice to pursue my entrepreneurial dreams. I was young, naive (I'm from a small island with less than 100K people), no family money or connections. I pretty much worked 1-2 jobs during college.

I thought about doing my MBA. My then mentor, Dean Lewis Temares of Engineering at my university, suggested that I interview a few of the professors in the MBA program. Let's just say, after interviewing my would-be professors and realizing they 'talked' but had never really 'walked,' I was like.. yeah. No thanks.

The one thing I had going for me at graduation was 6 job offers. Amidst a 2.84 GPA, which was the limit for computer engineers, as a part of the National Society of Black Engineers, I managed to get offers from companies like Caterpillar and General Mills. This was in part due to an e-book I bought online that suggested I put my low GPA on page 2 of my resume, in font size 8, and make sure I have a clear pitch before they (recruiters) ever eyeball my resume, with the hope they never turn the page! It worked!

How did you end up starting BI Brainz?

Yuk began a string of independent consulting jobs, which eventually led her to form her own company, BI Brainz. Since 2014, Yuk has been the CEO and Co-Founder of the company. The company specializes in helping Fortune 500 companies create actionable story-driven data visualizations to drive decision making. To do this, she created the BI Dashboard Formula methodology.

"I started as an independent consultant working for BusinessObjects, which is now owned by SAP. I went from having fun creating data visualizations in a tool called Xcelsius, to becoming the chick that fixed big problems. I was assigned to these big companies where executives complaints would be the same, 'I paid millions for this data warehouse and software, but I still have nothing to show.' So, I would give them something to show! A sexy data visualization with some detailed reports, turning the projects around within weeks, and then I would be moved unto the next unhappy C-level executive.

When SAP acquired BusinessObjects, they shut down the online community without notice, so I started my own online community EverythingXcelsius.com. Desperate for support, customers started contacting me through the blog. This is literally how our company started. There is a bit of a joke I tell sometimes. When I started my blog, and big companies emailed us, I thought they were hackers from a foreign country trying to get us to send them money!

One-hundred percent of our lead generation came from word of mouth or social media. Our company evolved out of necessity. We didn't have a company website for almost three years. Our customers asked us to get a website so they could refer us."

Yuk believes strongly that actionable and appealing data visualizations are a great asset to a company's data science program. Data-driven cultures thrive when companies can visualize and use their data in a more effective way. Yuk seeks to help her clients utilize data visualizations in a way that allows them to tell a story. Her clients are diverse; Ericsson, Bank of America, Shell, Qatargas, Nestle, Allstate, Webcor, and FedEx are just a few of her customers.

BI Brainz offers a range of services meant to help companies improve the visibility and use of every aspect of their data via analytics. They identify the specific areas where companies can improve using a technique she calls 'data visual storyboarding.' BI Brainz helps their clients improve everything, from merely updating their data visualization and reports to more abstract functions like creating data stories based on a specific use case, and then communicating it in a way that anyone can understand. BI Brainz helps companies renovate their existing visualization products, or they can dig deeper and help them formulate a new strategy that will allow the company culture to shift towards a more data-driven outlook. Yuk offers her expertise in taking existing data and helping clients uncover the hidden stories beneath the numbers.

What were some of the keys to your success early in your career?

"Taking risks - though some were very impulsive and not so smart in retrospect. After much debate, and without a plan, I called my 6 job offers a few weeks after my college graduation and declined them all via phone in a single batch. In my mind, I wanted to be an entrepreneur. I don't know where I read it... but some book stated that if I got 'hooked on the W2 drug', I would never come off of it. At the age of 23, that was enough to scare me. I was afraid to be like everyone else.

My mentor - Dean Lewis Temares of our Engineering school, and back then rated top CIO in the world was my mentor. I would waltz into his office and bounce my ideas of where I wanted to go and listen as he provided candid feedback. We still talk today! He's like my second dad.

More exposure - I kept throwing myself into different types of 'events' and 'internships' in college. I worked on South Beach for a very wealthy family who owned lots of hotels. I also volunteered on the weekend to help recovering drug addicts gain computer skills so they could find jobs to support their families. I participated in different conferences and even started some online businesses. When I dropped out of college, I spent 4-6 hours each day in Barnes and Nobles in the self-help section... I just wanted to learn. I was addicted to reading self-help books and biographies. I eventually graduated 6 and 1/2 years later."

The BI Dashboard Formula Methodology & more

Over time, Yuk has been able to develop her own formula to improve data visualization. No matter what platform a company is using, Yuk has streamlined a strategy to achieve the same results. She calls this the BI Dashboard Formula Methodology. By moving companies through this process, BI Brainz helps them choose appropriate BI projects, saving time and money. Once they choose a platform for the data visualization, the company walks through the process to choose the most actionable key performance indicators. The formula includes a process for building the right stories for the right audience and translating that into visually appealing analytics. Yuk is always interested in improving the use of data visualizations, and she works to socialize and humanize them.

On top of being able to build dashboards from the ground up, Yuk can assess the products that a company is already using. Yuk and her BI Brainz team are able to determine the data maturity of companies quickly. By doing assessments of the type of analytics that companies already have in place, they can improve what is already there rather than build entirely new systems.

Under Yuk's leadership, BI Brainz offers large companies two options, one is a consulting subscription-based model, and the other is via private corporate training to upskill their team on the BI Dashboard Formula methodology. Most customers do both. BI Brainz has multiple success stories with companies like University of Nebraska, Mobile Mini, and Qatargas. The BI Brainz Academy also offers free webinars, a student community, and a broad offering of online courses.

Social media and giving back to the community

Yuk has maximized her contribution to big data in a number of ways. In addition to her consulting business and academy, she engages on multiple topics about data science. Named number eight of the twenty-five entrepreneur influencers in BI, Yuk maintains a hearty social media presence. In the podcast and blog Analytics on Fire, Yuk dishes out all kinds of tidbits aimed to help improve the use of dashboards and data visualization. Her collaboration with leaders in the big data industry is always user-friendly and energetic.

She also keynotes globally at major industry events. Last year she spoke at the Real Business Intelligence event, held at MIT she shared a talk about her expertise – telling stories from data and was rated as the #1 speaker! She was able to explain the importance of not just presenting data but presenting it well. She was not shy about sharing her most effective practices concerning sharing the stories contained within data, and she challenged every listener to improve their metrics and data visualizations.

Yuk also delivered a 10-minute opening keynote, TED-talk style at Google Black Tech Mecca event which took over the number one trending spot on Twitter in Chicago for three minutes during her opening. She presented data that showed the lack of minority representation in technology (less than 2%). Additionally, a year later Yuk spoke at the first Facebook Women in Analytics event as the only founder using data to show the anemic investment in women startups which stand at 1.9% of all venture capital (VC) funding.

Yuk also authored a practical how-to book called *Data Visualization for Dummies*. This guide to data visualization breaks down the technical aspects of data visualization into easy steps. The book presents tips for synthesizing complicated data into good stories tailored to a target audience. Throughout the text, Yuk emphasizes the idea that too much data can overwhelm the audience, and she explains how the visualizations should be used judiciously for maximum benefits.

Yuk has also created an online course called BI Data Storytelling Mastery; she is hyper-focused on developing Chief Data Storytellers in organizations. The course is designed to teach others how to easily set up, build and design their first compelling data story. The course helps to eliminate the need for dashboard design skills, removes the difficulties of gathering requirements, and puts an end to building useless reports.

Why do most business intelligence projects fail?

Yuk is perplexed that according to Gartner, 85% of all big data project fail (as of Nov 2017) while business intelligence software spend will be a projected $187B by 2020. Gartner also stated that only 30% of all business intelligence projects were successful (Nov 2017). That means that companies are investing considerable amounts of time, energy, and millions of dollars into projects that may not return the investment. Yuk advises executives to view data as an asset rather than a technological investment. When used to drive decisions it can be the difference between a Netflix and a Blockbuster. She also feels that instead of spending so much money on just technology, companies should re-allocate at least 20% of that budget to upskill and add new talent to their data teams. Another 10% should be spent on upgrading the user experience of their existing analytics to build user trust.

"Business intelligence projects must be managed properly to gain measurable ROI. Here are some of the top factors that might cause your analytics endeavors to fall short:

1. *No Executive Buy-in - No complex project succeeds without executive buy-in. Sadly, many companies seem to forget this golden rule when it comes to BI, and their projects either outright fail or go off in the wrong direction.*

2. *Old Technology - Technologies like SAP and Oracle were once at the forefront of business intelligence and analytics. While these platforms still have applications in provisioning and ERP, their roots lie in decades-old business models and technological standards that weren't designed with the cloud in mind. Workflows are changing, and BI technology needs to keep up. Build your projects around tools that incorporate data visualization, mobile accessibility, and drag-and-drop reports right out of the box, as almost all of today's standalone BI products do.*

3. *Lack of Business Support - One Gartner global manager noted that a lack of business support and training was a common culprit in the failure of BI projects. No matter how much information you create, failing to communicate with team members and enact actionable response mechanisms will render your data ineffective. Business intelligence projects aren't just for managers. They ought to represent company-wide efforts to make changes, so make sure everyone is on board from the beginning, and implement training that helps workers play their part by tracking relevant data."*

Yuk's BI Dashboard Methodology takes all of these factors into account and sets up a clear plan to tackle each one based on her years of experience as a top-tier consultant.

In a field where Ph.D.'s are commonplace; you achieved great success without obtaining one. What do you think lead to that success?

"It depends on how you define success. It can't be solely based on education. I had 6 job offers after college with a 2.84 GPA in engineering, which was twice as many offers as my classmates with 4.0 GPAs. How? I Googled 'How to get a job with a low GPA' and downloaded an eBook from some whiz kid who landed the job of his dreams with a 1.6 GPA and was then a financial broker on Wall Street. I followed his tactics down to the 't.' Also, going to college at 16 was great. I had two years to experiment and still make it out on time (age wise). However, if where I

am today both personally and professionally is the bar for success, it's a combination of faith, curiosity, and passion.

Faith - I come from a fairly religious background. We are Jewish, so we do Shabbat and the high holidays. Regardless of the outcome, I have faith that everything happens for a reason (Ephesian 3) and God has a plan, even if I don't know all of it today... He didn't bring me this far to fail. I have had to remind myself of this many times.

Curiosity - I was blessed to have parents who never told me there was a box. We were never told that we were different than anyone else, rich or poor. Therefore, in my head, there were no boundaries when it came to success. If one door closes, there are many others open... you have to find them. The Kentucky Fried Chicken story always comes to mind. 1009 no's but the one yes that changed everything."

Here's a brief story of Colonel Harland Sanders and Kentucky Fried Chicken: Col. Sanders was a fellow who really loved to share his fried chicken recipe. He had a lot of positive influence from those who tasted the chicken. Now, the Colonel was retired and up in age and while most people believed in the sanctimony of retirement, the Colonel opted to sell the world on his cool new chicken recipe. With little in terms of means at his disposal, Col. Sanders traveled door to door to houses and restaurants all over his local area. He wanted to partner with someone to help promote his chicken recipe. Needless to say, he was met with little enthusiasm.

He started travelling by car to different restaurants and cooked his fried chicken on the spot for restaurant owners. If the owner liked the chicken, they would enter into a handshake agreement to sell the Colonel's chicken. Legend has it that Colonel Sanders heard 1009 "no"s before he heard his first "yes". Basically, he was turned down one-thousand and nine times before his chicken was accepted once!

"I should also note that my best ideas come from sitting in the bookstore, on the floor, reading. Whenever I am stuck, I resort back to this. I also never stop

learning! I listen to two podcasts minimum a day during my morning shower and exercise, and I journal and read for 20 minutes a day.

Passion - I love art and computers. Remember those 6 job offers? Most of them were for a 'program analyst' role. I couldn't see myself coding all day, though at the time I could code in 12 languages. Passion is important, as it led me to start my blog 'Analytics on Fire,' get on Twitter, launch my online course, and continue to share my experience around the world in my keynotes and training. During my 'drop out phase,' in college, I read the following few quotes that have stuck with me to this day:

'Do what you love, and the money will follow' Marsha Sinetar, Do What You Love, the Money Will Follow: Discovering Your Right Livelihood

'You can get everything in life you want if you will just help enough people get what they want.' Zig Ziglar, Secrets of Closing the Sale (1984)

I also learned from Malcolm Gladwell's book Outliers; it takes 10,000 hours to become an expert. If I stayed behind a desk coding, I knew that I would not cross the 100-hour mark.

By the way, I am not successful. In my opinion, I have yet to reach my 10-year goal. Remember where I talked about dropping out of college and sitting in the bookstore? Well, one of the books I read stated that writing down goals was key... they also said broke people plan day-to-day, average people plan yearly, but visionaries and the super successful plan in five and ten-year spans. They always look forward. I still have that goal sheet I created at age 20, and I keep it up to date using W.I.G.S. (wildly important goals)."

Advocate for diversity

Yuk acknowledges that it is not easy being a passionate leader. The fact that she is both black and a woman poses obstacles. Despite the challenges, Yuk passionately advocates for diversity in her industry, and, as the head of her international consulting firm, she is a persuasive advocate. She has keynoted events like Google's Black Tech Mecca. Google runs this event, and its purpose is to empower minorities and bring diversity to the technology industry by using data. Yuk showcased data that tells a sad, but true, story about the state of diversity in the technology industry. Of all the blacks in the United States, fewer than 1% have jobs in the industry. Yuk wants to be able to mentor and lead others, encouraging them to enter the field and change that statistic.

Yuk also advocates for women in leadership positions. She is very aware of her power as an influencer, and she uses it in positive ways. Not only does she promote women in technology through her social media presence, but she also takes the time to mentor women who are striving to be leaders in their careers. With a little research, it is easier than ever to find examples of others who are having success in any given field.

What advice would you give to other women who are interested in pursuing a similar career path to yours?

"Do it.

Data is the new oil.

Data is the new currency.

With data, the sky is the limit, as the uses and applications of data are infinite. Data, like the internet, will drive every facet of our lives. Think of it as getting a free ride to Mars!"

What can women in the workplace do today to help build the foundation for successful careers?

"Defy gravity. That is what I strive to do. I was blessed to grow up in the Caribbean, where my parents never told me there was a box. I saw no barriers. I always encourage the women I mentor to look at the opportunities, not the challenges. Give the benefit of the doubt to those ignorant of the challenges we face. Seek out those around you who may need help. Join external networking groups like Women 2.0 or She++ to keep close tabs with like-minded women. We know that as women

we have to work harder, so instill it into your mindset. Don't be average. Exceed expectations and take on new challenges. I'm tired of hearing about the lack of opportunities. After working with 50+ large global companies, you'd be surprised to see how many men will help to champion our cause. We're in an era where many men in this field have daughters and have finally realized that unless they help to create the change, their daughters will face the same challenges we do. Don't limit your support channels."

What are some of the biggest challenges that you can identify for data scientists in the future?

"Technology & Trust - As we speak, the role of 'data engineer' has almost triple the number of job postings as 'data scientist.' As technology evolves, and everything, including algorithms, become a commodity, their role may have to change. People want data science, but they also want control. Today, having both is difficult.

Data Variety & Velocity - As data grows, unfortunately, so does the problem of data velocity. I see this as being a continuous problem. If you build an algorithm, it can easily be garbage in and garbage out. See Cathy O'Neil's book - Weapons of Math Destruction. Data scientist need to figure out what data makes sense to keep first and foremost."

Yuk is a true example of a person breaking through barriers. As a woman of color and a data scientist, Yuk has contributed fiercely and passionately to the field. Not only does she offer key technical insight into a niche area of data visualization and storytelling, but she is a mentor and leader as well.

MONICA ROGATI

DATA SCIENCE AND AI ADVISOR; EQUITY PARTNER AT DCVC

"These days, I'm more motivated by the impact computer science has on our lives as we face a similar paradigm shift: steering technology towards desired outcomes by carefully defining them, with an eye towards fairness and avoiding unintended consequences."

Monica Rogati brings technical expertise, academic pedigree, and a superlative resume to the table. Her academic experience is combined with her real-world experience, making her a formidable practitioner of data science.

What inspired you to study computer science and technology?

"The first computer I used was one with no permanent storage (so everything had to be loaded or programmed from scratch every time) and no graphical interface. If you were lucky, you could load a simple game by using a cassette player – but most of the time, you just had to type everything in BASIC, the first computer language I've learned.

It might sound tedious and boring, but, believe it or not, it felt like magic. Being able to teach a machine to draw a complex geometric pattern, find prime numbers, compose a simple song, guess a number or an animal, play a simple game – it all felt like magic. I've always loved puzzles, and figuring out how to break this complex behavior into its simplest, well-defined components was fascinating and thrilling.

That feeling stuck with me as I grew up and learned how to build more complex algorithms and eventually used data and machine learning to steer the computer towards a desired behavior instead of giving it those step-by-step instructions I remembered from childhood.

These days, I'm more motivated by the impact computer science has on our lives as we face a similar paradigm shift: steering technology towards desired outcomes by carefully defining them, with an eye towards fairness and avoiding unintended consequences."

Early life and college

Born in Romania, Rogati began her journey by attending Tudor Vianu National College of Computer Science, which was a secondary school that focused on preparing students for careers in Information Technology. She then went on to the University of New Mexico, where she completed a Bachelor's of Science degree in Computer

Science. Rogati's performance at the University of New Mexico was superlative. She graduated first in her class in a challenging field where she had researched neural networks and natural language processing. From there, she earned both a master's degree and a PhD in Computer Science at the well-known Carnegie Mellon University. Her thesis topic foreshadowed her future career in data science, as it was titled "Domain Adaptation of Translation Models for Multilingual Applications."

Working at LinkedIn

From Carnegie Mellon, Rogati began her rise in the field of data science by working at LinkedIn. This was a perfect place to begin her career because the company was one of the first to have entire teams doing data science tasks. In fact, DJ Patil, one of the individuals credited with coining the term 'data scientist,' worked at LinkedIn during Rogati's tenure with the company. It was a perfect time and place for Rogati to begin innovating.

During her five-year tenure at LinkedIn, from 2008 to 2013, she contributed several now well-known features to the website. Using her technical expertise, she designed one of the first versions of the website's feature that matches individuals with potential jobs. She developed the first machine learning model for the feature that shows 'People You May Know' on the website. She also worked on the features of Talent Match and Groups You May Like. She even contributed in less flashy, but equally important, ways for detecting fraud. She helped the company identify fake accounts and worked to eliminate spam and terms of services (TOS) violations.

What was the most challenging part of moving from the academic setting where you had earned a PhD into the corporate world?

"Moving from academia to industry required a shift in mindset, best summarized in this tweet:

Monica Rogati ✔
@mrogati

Easy test for CS PhDs deciding on academia
vs. industry:
When a simple method works, do you a)
curse or b) celebrate?

6:52 PM · 27 Jun 2011

*I was used to exploring one particular aspect in depth and pursuing the limit of what's theoretically possible. After many years of being trained that discovering new, better algorithms is what's important and what your academic career depends on, it can be hard to switch gears. In industry, I quickly realized that it's more impactful to use simple, proven methods to take a solution from 0% to 80% and then move on to a different problem that sits at 0% -- because you're optimizing for customer impact. I've also deeply internalized the concept of opportunity cost: what project *isn't* getting done while you're working on this?*

Your time is your most valuable resource. In academia, spending months researching and implementing a more sophisticated, publishable solution that leads to a 5-10% improvement is a big success -- and that's by design, since you are pushing the boundaries of knowledge. In industry (and especially in startups), quickly implementing an effective baseline and moving on to the next project that's sitting at 0% is a better use of your time."

What attracted you to the job at LinkedIn?

"Team, data, impact. I joined LinkedIn in early 2008, when it had a little over 200 employees (last time I checked, that number hovered around 10,000). I was coming out of academia, and I was impressed by the team — they were knowledgeable, friendly, and happy to answer all my naive questions: What's a 'datamart' and how is that different from a database? What's 'production'? ETL? Why are you calling a portion of the web page a 'product'?

LinkedIn's data was unique in scope and size — 17 million members and their career histories (it's more than half a billion now). The labor market insights we've found in that data were incredible (or just fun): how industries evolve, how job titles changed over decades, best time of the year to get a promotion, what makes entrepreneurs different – and the most successful first names. This work continues to this day, formalized as the monthly LinkedIn Workforce Report.

As an early LinkedIn member, I was already very excited about its mission and impact on people's careers and economic opportunities. But my personal impact looked very promising, too: machine learning wasn't being used yet, and my background in NLP and applied ML was going to be put to good use immediately. That's rare for fresh PhDs, and having a practical, immediate impact at scale (and as part of a high-performing team) was even rarer. I was thrilled to join."

While eliminating fake accounts may not sound like a glamorous task, Rogati points out how erroneous or fake data can skew the big picture. If fake accounts are considered in features like People You May Know, then the feature is failing. Additionally, the fake accounts can mislead data scientists. How can we determine which jobs are really that popular if the information collected is not from legitimate profiles? Rogati often emphasizes the importance of basic functions like data cleaning to prevent problems like those caused by fake accounts.

Working with interesting and unique data

On top of doing the technical work that required complex computations, Rogati connected the hard facts with softer stories. She was able to identify interesting information that she gleaned from the data. While LinkedIn had collected information about the lives of over 120 million people, it was not always so obvious how that information could be aggregated and shared in useful (or interesting) ways. Using LinkedIn's data about people's career histories, Rogati found interesting patterns that were published as articles in top news outlets such as The Wall Street Journal and The Economist. These stories included topics like "overused buzzwords" and "top times of the year to be promoted." This synthesis of data, which is now commonplace, was being presented to the public in new ways under her leadership at LinkedIn.

It was at this job that Rogati found herself learning to ask the questions that define data scientists. She learned to ask what information was needed, and then she learned to ask what algorithm had to be developed to get that information.

Importance of effective communication

Rogati became highly proficient at communicating that data to others. Another critical piece of her work at LinkedIn involved sharing her innovation with others. Rogati organized a series of technical talks, and she assisted with a summer internship program that gave participants experience in the new field of data science. As with many of the other big data experts, sharing knowledge and preparing people to enter the field is an important role for Rogati.

Moving on to Jawbone

From her position at LinkedIn, she moved on to Jawbone, a company that focused on building wearable fitness products. Rogati served as the Vice President of Data at the company from July 2013 until June 2015. During this time, Rogati was in charge of building the Jawbone data science team. The functions that the team developed for the wearable fitness trackers were groundbreaking. Using data from the device, the team developed applications to personalize its output. The fitness trackers became smarter in the sense that they began recognizing what actions the user was (or was not) taking. Using the data it was collecting, the device could remind the wearer to get active or the device could autonomously begin tracking exercise.

Along with the different activity-tracking features of the device, the users could also monitor a variety of different things that impact health, including sleep, nutrition, weight, and heart rate. The wearable fitness tracker was able to bring data visualization to the user at faster rates than ever before. While developing this technology, Rogati looked for ways to help individuals input their data (like meals or water consumption). She knew that by improving functions like autocomplete, the wearer would be more apt to enter information into the application and then benefit from the data collected. These small improvements lead to more data and better quality in the long run, which, in the case of wearable fitness trackers, should help the user improve his or her health.

Becoming an advisor

Now, Rogati serves as an independent data science advisor and fractional data executive. She serves her clients in the fields of data science and artificial intelligence. Rogati prides herself with helping clients fully utilize their data. Not only does she want companies to be able to have the technical expertise to access and compile their data, but she also advocates for the strategic use of that data.

What are some of your current projects?

"As a fractional data executive and advisor, I work with many companies on technical and strategic projects. They all vary from company to company, but we're focusing on the impact data science can have on the company and its field."

Inspired by Abraham Maslow

Recently, Rogati has proposed new ideas to help companies understand the broad range of data science functions. Through her illustration, she reminds companies that the basics of data science should not be neglected in favor of fancier technology. In order to explain the need for a range of data science functions, Rogati took inspiration from Abraham Maslow. Maslow famously theorized that humans were motivated by a series of different needs. The essence of his theory is that humans seek to fulfill basic, concrete needs like food, shelter, and clothing before they seek more abstract needs, and the theory is often visualized as a pyramid, with the more basic needs listed at the bottom and the more abstract needs on top. Rogati proposes a similar concept for companies. She posits that while many companies are concerned about AI and Deep Learning, there are a multitude of other, more basic data science issues that should be addressed before focusing on those two more complex topics.

At the base of her 'data science hierarchy of needs,' Rogati lists a general group of functions that focuses on collection of data. These functions can include logging, sensors, and external data. While these functions are not nearly as glamorous as AI or Deep Learning, they serve a crucial purpose for companies wanting to improve the use of data. Moving up from the collection functions are functions that include the movement or storage of data. These functions include data storage and data flow. Beyond the movement or storage of data, there are functions concerned with exploring and transformation of the data. This can involve cleaning the data, detecting anomalies, and preparing the data for different uses.

Beyond exploring and transforming data, there is the aggregation and labeling of data. Analytics and metrics play a large role in this layer of the pyramid. The next-to-last layer of Rogati's pyramid involves learning and optimizing data. A/B testing, experimentation, and simple ML algorithms help achieve those tasks. Only after all of those different layers does one finally arrive at AI and Deep Learning, at the pinnacle of the pyramid. This is a lesson that we should all take to heart: master the basics before focusing on more complex tasks.

Who were some of your mentors as you began working in the field of data science?

"I've learned a lot from everybody on the early LinkedIn team, especially Jay Kreps, Jonathan Goldman, DJ Patil, Ellen Levy, and Daniel Tunkelang. But I met my first data science mentor at AT&T Research, where I interned between my undergrad and PhD. Her name is Marilyn Walker, now a professor at UC Santa Cruz; we worked on machine learning for dialogue systems. The year was 2000, and this topic was decades ahead of its time. Not only did she teach me the latest

machine learning methods, but I learned about doing research, collaborating with senior researchers, writing papers, and, most importantly, being part of a team where your contributions are valued and recognized."

Advice to aspiring data scientists

Rogati has practical advice for those wanting to enter the field of data science. *"Since this is a relatively new role and there's no universal agreement on what a data scientist does, it's difficult for a beginner to know where to start, and it's easy to get overwhelmed.*

I recommend building up a public portfolio of simple, but interesting projects. If getting a job as a data scientist is a priority, this portfolio will open many doors, and if your topic, findings or product are interesting to a broader audience, you'll have more incoming recruiting calls than you can handle."

Below are the steps Rogati recommends. They are optimized for maximizing learning and chances to get a data job.

1. Select a topic that you are curious about. *"Research what datasets are available out there, or datasets you could create or obtain with minimal effort and expense."* The goal here is to be able to answer exciting questions or to build something interesting.

2. Write the tweet first. This is Rogati's take on forming the hypothesis as part of the scientific method (in the 21st century). *"You'll probably never actually tweet this, and you probably think tweets are a frivolous avenue to disseminate scientific findings. But it's essential that you write 1–2 sentences about your (hypothetical) findings *before* you start.*

Here are a few examples, with a conversational hook thrown in:

"I used LinkedIn data to find out what makes entrepreneurs different—it turns out they're older than you think, and they tend to major in physics but not in nursing or theology. I guess it's hard to get VC funding to start your own religion."

"I used Jawbone data to see how weather affects activity levels—it turns out people in NY are less sensitive to weather variations than Californians. Do you think New Yorkers are tougher or just work out indoors?"

"I combined BBC obituary data with Wikipedia entries to see if 2016 was as bad as we thought for celebrities."

Rogati goes on to say, that the aspiring data scientist should visualize themselves repeating this 'tweet' or hypothesis at job interviews or even this being posted in a Wall Street Journal story. *"Are you boring yourself and having trouble explaining it, or do you feel proud and smart? If the answer is "meh", repeat step 2 (and possibly 1) until you have 2–3 compelling ideas. Get feedback from others—does this sound interesting? Would you interview somebody who built this for a data job?"*

Since at this stage you haven't actually done any programming work it is easier to rethink your approach. *"It sounds obvious, but people are eager to jump into a random tutorial or class to feel productive and soon sink months into a project that is going nowhere."*

3. Do the work. At this stage Rogati states that the data needs to be explored, cleaned, graphed and analyzed. *"Look at the top 10 most frequent values for each column. Study the outliers. Check the distributions. Group similar values if it's too fragmented. Look for correlations and missing data. Try various clustering and classification algorithms. Debug. Learn why they worked or didn't on your data. Build data pipelines on AWS if your data is big. Try various NLP libraries on your unstructured text data. Yes, you might learn Spark, numpy, pandas, nltk, matrix factorization and TensorFlow—not to check a box next to a laundry list, but because you *need* it to accomplish something you care about. Be a detective. Come up with new questions and unexpected directions. See if things make sense. Did you find a giant issue with how the data was collected? What if you bring in another data set? Ride the data wave. This should feel exciting and fun, with the occasional roadblock. Get help and feedback online, from Kaggle, from mentors if*

you have access to them, or from a buddy doing the same thing. If this does not feel like fun, go back to step 1. If the thought of that makes you hate life, reconsider being a data scientist: this is as fun as it gets, and you won't be able to sustain the hard work and the 80% drudgery of a real data job if you don't find this part energizing.)"

4. Communicate. An integral part of the process is to document your findings in a language that can be easily understood, accompanies by clean and crisp visualizations. *"You'll learn several data visualization tools in the process, which I highly recommend (it's an underrated investment in your skills). Have a clean, interesting demo or video if you built a prototype. Technical details and code should be a link away. Send it around and get feedback. This being public will hold yourself to a higher standard and will result in good quality code, writing and visualizations."*

After you follow these four steps, and repeat with other datasets, you will have likely learned about several of the latest technologies and have a portfolio of projects that you can share with hiring managers. *"Send a link to the hiring manager on your dream data science team. When you get the job, send me a Sterling Truffle Bar."*

Data science influencer

Rogati is an influencer on social media. She was recently featured in an article describing ten data science experts that you could follow on Twitter. Her expertise in AI and ML are two of things that attract followers, and, speaking of followers, she has amassed a hefty 45K on Twitter.

Rogati will continue to be a leader in the industry. Her expertise and experience will continue to foment innovations in the field, and her message of mastering the basics before moving on to more challenging functions is one that both new data scientists and more experienced practitioners can apply.

NATALIE EVANS HARRIS

CO-FOUNDER AND COO OF BRIGHTHIVE

"When data is responsibly and ethically used for social services, it can drive social equity from government services to individual communities. The convergence of our digital and physical selves requires a culture that encourages questioning how data is collected, analyzed and used. We need data scientists to have more options than staying quiet, quitting, or whistle-blowing when they see something that isn't right."

In the world of data scientists, Natalie Evans Harris brings a fresh viewpoint to the conversation. As a successful African-American woman hailing from the Bronx and a former long-time employee of one of the nation's largest data collecting agencies (the National Security Agency, or NSA), she helps draw attention to underrepresented groups in the data industry.

While her roots are in New York City, as the daughter of an Air Force man, Evans Harris attended school in Delaware and Maryland. She has a diverse academic background, earning two bachelor's degrees from the University of Maryland Eastern Shore, one in sociology and one in computer science. These two degrees speak volumes about both the expertise and the service-oriented nature of this remarkable woman. Throughout her career, she would leverage her data expertise to effect positive changes for the people whose data was at stake.

In addition to undergraduate degrees, Evans Harris also earned a degree in Public Administration from George Washington University in Washington, D.C. This degree would help lay the foundation for her excellent work with the NSA.

How did you end up in data science?

"When I went to college, I knew I wanted to do something to improve governments support of communities. I wanted to become a lawyer to help make these changes and promote equality. I knew the way to make an impact is by changing the policies that drive these decisions and actions.

I wanted to become the first African-American, female, Supreme Court Justice until I got my first job on campus as IT Support. My first job on campus was laying the computer network cables. This introduced me to computers. This was my first deep technical experience with computers. I also worked at the IT helpdesk; this allowed me to see the different things we could do with networks, computers, and the Internet. Combining this with my sociology background, I decided to look at this intersection between community and society, individuals and technology. I realized that change doesn't happen by providing technology. People need the data and information that it can deliver to help make decisions.

I was recruited out of college by the NSA. I didn't know much about the NSA at the time. I was excited that I had a job and they were going to pay for my graduate school tuition. I saw that they were using technology to drive change. They were doing this to support militaries. I thought I would stay there for a few years and then leave for something else. I ended up working for the NSA for 16 years, and it shaped my values on the value of data and the importance of being responsible data stewards. I joined the NSA 3 months before the September 11th crisis. At this point, everything changed; the focus shifted to applying my skills to helping our military and protecting our borders.

I didn't know I was a data scientist until about 10 years into my career, when 'data science' became a thing. I had a career to use data responsibly to drive decisions."

Career at National Security Agency (NSA)

For over 16 years, Evans Harris served our nation as a manager in this public institution (NSA). Her work there would be formative in her current pursuits outside the Federal Government. The mission of the NSA is to collect intelligence data concerning other foreign countries and determine how best to protect the security of the United States. Balancing how to collect massive amounts of data while respecting the civil liberties of the American public. It is in this atmosphere of constantly balancing individual rights against national security that Natalie Evans Harris began her professional career.

During her tenure at the NSA, Evans Harris had the opportunity to lead a team in designing and implementing a data science immersion program for hiring and onboarding data science talent. She recognized that some of the traditional hiring requirements such as requiring a STEM degree not only restricted the candidate pool for data scientists but also neglected the importance of other analytic and inter-personal skills. Preventing her from hiring some strong candidates with non-technical (or self-taught technical) skills and strong analytical skills. Through the data science immersion program, she encouraged different methods for assessing the practical skills of potential employees before hiring them. By focusing on skills rather than degrees, Evans Harris was able to affect the diversity and onboarding practices to reflect the diversity and complexity of the agency's data science needs. She implemented methods that tested the applicants' skills in practical scenarios. These methods became a permanent part of the agency's practices in hiring data scientists.

Much of her work in the NSA dealt with making data actionable, but Evans Harris was also in tune with the skills needed to drive the organization. She gained valuable experience in the different aspects of the NSA's mission by filling key project management and organizational leadership positions. Her performance was so impressive that she was able to earn a Brookings Legislative Fellowship and work for Senator Cory Booker. This fellowship gave her an opportunity to view the workings of the legislative process firsthand. These fellowships often help create connections and allow participants to directly engage in the work of the legislature. Evans Harris spent her year focusing on topics that had become important to her, cybersecurity, privacy, and workforce development. She leveraged her expertise to advise on policy and the tough technical issues that faced the Cyber Information Security Protection Act (CISPA).

While CISPA was never passed, it served as the forerunner of another piece of legislation, the Cybersecurity Information Sharing Act (CISA). This latter piece of legislation was proposed in order to facilitate the United States Government's ability to protect its cybersecurity through information-sharing. Specifically, the bill tried to foment the sharing of information between the government and private entities so that cyber threats could be proactively neutralized.

During the debate for these different pieces of legislation, the issue of civil liberties rose to the forefront. The Obama administration was concerned that the bill did not allow for protection of confidential information and did not adequately safeguard the civil liberties of individuals. President Obama promised to veto CISPA if the bill were passed. Being in the middle of this policy debate would prove to be another important experience for this tenacious woman.

Suffering from 'imposter syndrome'

"My whole career, in most situations, I've been the only one of me. NSA was a predominantly male, white community. It's no secret they have diversity problems in the intelligence community. I was (and still am) often the only African American, the only woman in a room. It has held true throughout my career. The last few years when I worked under the Obama administration, it's changed some, but I still feel different, think different. I have to fight hard to remember that different doesn't mean wrong and I have something valuable to contribute. It still blows my mind when people ask me to speak at a conference.

I've embraced the fact that I think differently, and to not be afraid to be wrong sometimes. I got over the fear of being wrong or being exposed as not the smartest in the room. I've been trying to accept my diversity as an asset, being purposeful in identifying how it adds value while acclimating to my environments. I try not to over-acclimate and miss opportunities to improve diversity and inclusion, but it's a balancing act. At the same time, I don't want to alienate the people I need to collaborate with. I've been fortunate to be surrounded by people that encouraged me to be comfortable with who I am."

What advice do you have for minorities in this space?

"Being an individual and being diverse and thoughtful and bringing unique experience to a situation is so critical to the success of data science for social good. Find ways to bring diversity of thought together. Don't just focus on algorithms and the science. Think of how the data is actually used and beyond your objectives, what are the unintended consequences.

If you are driving decisions with data, then you need to understand where it comes from and what it can and can't tell you. The connection between data science, community impact, and improving the lives of minorities is not always obvious. Pursuing data science to help our (minorities') communities is not often a dream pursued because the connection to the institutional bias we experience every day is not obvious."

This piece of history helps to bring home the point: Ida B Wells was a pioneering data scientist during the civil rights movement who collected and used data to prove that black people were lynched more often for infractions such as failing to pay debts, not appearing to give way to whites, and competing with whites economically. She found little basis for the frequent claim that black men were lynched because they had sexually abused or attacked white women. Publishing this data served as momentum for gathering support from the educated African-American community and challenged white America's collective acceptance or silence on lynching. While she soon realized that data alone won't drive change, her investigative journalism and other efforts as a leader of the Civil Rights Movement all used data as a motivator.

"The promises of technology to make everything better in our lives, to be the great equalizer, has not only exacerbated the biases and inequalities that are ingrained in American culture, but also created dependencies, addictions, and born the most questionable, immoral, behaviors, leaving us with this ethical dilemma.

Does the good outweigh the bad? The blurred line between who we are as individuals, and our digital presence, is forcing everyone to question what role data has in delivering technology that measurably benefits rather than abuse those that social services intend to support the most; we now have to treat data and digital services differently than how we have treated technology to-date. It's not about the innovation but rather about how we treat individuals even in their digital state. How do we assess and prioritize ethics/societal impact above innovation? The power is not in the data itself, but in how the data is used."

Working at the White House

Evans Harris continued her service to the American people by becoming part of the Obama administration's emphasis on improving the Federal government's capacity to increase opportunity through data. In January 2016, Evans Harris became the Senior Policy Advisor to the United States Chief Technology Officer and first US Chief Data Scientist. This appointment was part of a larger push by the administration to unlock the power of data. President Obama had a vision to improve the data capabilities of the U.S. government, which owns some of the largest amounts of data in the world. The administration worked to recruit government outsiders from places like Silicon Valley as well as experts who had excelled in different government agencies.

Even though she didn't come from Silicon Valley, Evans Harris was a perfect choice for leading institutional data transformation in the federal government. She brought her expertise in data collection, analysis, and safeguarding from her work at the NSA. She also knew how to successfully navigate federal bureaucracy, since she had spent 16 years learning the ropes in the intelligence sector. The Bookings fellowship with Senator Booker completed her resume, giving her the policy-making experience that would serve her well in the new position.

Evans Harris began building concrete processes to improve the government's use of data. She strove to establish guidance on best practices for the new area of expertise by founding the Data Cabinet. The Data Cabinet is a monthly meeting of key federal players in the data sciences field. This group encompassed a prodigious 200 individuals that represented over 40 federal agencies. By bringing these leaders together on a regular basis, Evans Harris was able to harness the power of their organizational knowledge and identify the problems that were facing the federal government. Not only could the group identify the problems, but they were crucial in developing solutions to those problems. For the first time, policy makers could not only see the big picture of the data problems facing the United States government but collaboratively establish best practices for solving them.

"The Data Cabinet is something that I can hold up as an example of the impact of collective action. As a group, the Data Cabinet created several best practice tools,

but more importantly, it created a space for discussions, for conversations about the challenges of using data effectively."

She worked on projects that would have positive implications for the American worker. In a partnership with the University of Chicago and the Department of Labor, she created the Open Skills Community. This project was meant to deliver practical tools for the nation's workforce to understand training and employment opportunities. The Workforce Data Initiative became the vehicle to carry out this partnership. The goal was to bring information to the nation's workforce. Through the website dataatwork.org, developers and data scientists receive the foundational components for building a more open, connected, and interoperable workforce data ecosystem. At the heart of the issue, Evans Harris wanted to connect all the information and all the players in the fields of labor and education and give them the tools they need to determine what jobs exist in the marketplace and whether training and education are available to meet those needs. This work carried into her co-founding BrightHive to help States and local governments leverage these tools to connect their workforce communities.

Another formative project for Evans Harris during her tenure in the White House was joining the Opportunity Project. Launched in 2016 this project brought open-source government data together with application developers to create tools to empower individuals with the information and resources that would help them improve their economic situations. And again, Evans Harris worked with a diverse team to connect key players not only in the government but in the non-profit sector as well. Using government datasets and input from these stakeholders, she worked with government leaders and the Opportunity Project team to push for the development of 29 different tools aimed to work on real problems facing individuals, such as unemployment, underemployment, improving job skills, accessing transportation, and researching schools. These tools also provided more transparency for the American public. They are still being used to help individuals gain access to information about wages and civil rights issues.

What can be done to inspire others to launch conversations that can effect change?

"One of my favorite quotes from Barbara Jordan, first African-American Representative from Texas and first African-American to give keynote at 1976 Democratic National Convention, focused on this desire of people to make the world a better place. Even the most pessimistic still envision a change in society, they just doubt the reality of the change. Perhaps driven by my imposter syndrome, I believe everyone has a voice and ability to effect change in their own way. People live and breathe the change and with every speaking event, every workshop, everything I do I focus on not providing the answers, but empowering others to see a path for change within themselves and their communities."

> *'We are a people in a quandary about the present. We are a people in search of our future. We are a people in search of a national community... We are a people trying not only to solve the problems of the present, unemployment, inflation, but we are attempting on a larger scale to fulfill the promise of America... We are attempting to fulfill our national purpose, to create and sustain a society in which all of us are equal.'* - **Barbara Jordan**

"President Obama's Administration did a lot of great things for social change, but what was most remarkable for me was the growth of the civic tech community. A whole other book can be written about the impacts of this community (good and bad), but what cannot be disputed is the group represents the transformation of our society from one of hope - I hope he can do the things he says he's going to do - to one of we not only can but we will make the change. There isn't an innovation or impact from this Administration - from the ability to digitally report potholes, to advancements in healthcare, transportation, and our criminal justice system - that wasn't the result of different people from different sectors, backgrounds, and experiences coming together for a common purpose. The greatest legacy given to us was showing that changes happen through us.

The rise of digital attacks (hacks, identity theft, mis-information, etc.) and the increasing severity of those attacks on individual's financial security and civil liberties has forced the tech community to examine the moral fabric of innovation, of technology. Data ethics isn't just a technology issue, it's the outgrowth of a culture that seems to prioritize self-interest over community prosperity. Whether intentional or unintended, the outcome of putting innovation or profits, or individual gains, over the examination and protection of community is how we have arrived at this ethical dilemma. Unfortunately, change will not come in the hands of government or corporations. If you agree that the responsible/ethical use of data is a cultural problem, then it's important to recognize that government or corporations are rarely the source of solutions. The change happens when people decide enough is enough and then band together to drive those that can to make the change.

I want to see thoughts and behaviors changing because of conversations I've been involved in. I always want to see these things continue after I step away. I want to see other initiatives grow and other conversations happen, launched by other people. I haven't seen enough of that. I love bringing people together to have an impactful conversation that leads to action.

Community-driven Principles for Ethical Data Sharing (CPEDS)

The Community Principles on Ethical Data Practices (CPEDS) started as a conversation with Gideon Mann, Head of Data Science at Bloomberg, focused on defining ethical and responsible behaviors for sourcing, sharing and implementing data in a manner that will cause no harm and maximize positive impact. The goal of this initiative is to develop a community-driven code of ethics for data collection, sharing and utilization that provides people in the data science community a standard set of easily digestible, recognizable principles for guiding their behaviors.

"I launched the CPEDS initiative in Sept 2017 at Data for Good Exchange, with the idea that change happens when people decide enough is enough and then band together to drive the change.

For me, it started with creating a community that agreed on a set of principles and adopted those principles in a transparent way that allowed for ownership, accountability and proactive self-regulation. Together with Bloomberg (Thank you Gideon, Chaim, Susan and team!!) and Data For Democracy (Thank you

Jonathon, Mo, Margeaux, Astrid, David, and all the other volunteers!!) the CPEDS initiative grew to a community of over 800 data practitioners that recognize the gap in our capacity to drive change and agree collectively to create, highlight, provide the resources necessary for our community to be more ethical in the way data is used to drive innovation. Today, that community of practice exists within Data for Democracy as the Global Data Ethics Project. It's a community of volunteers that are being recognized for their expertise and collective impact.

My message to the public is 'you have a voice.' It's good to support others' initiatives, but find the space that you want to own. Understand the change you want to see and then bring together 4 friends to make it happen.' We need people to recognize their voice and their power to drive change."

Career post-government

In April 2017, Evans Harris left the federal government to pursue different opportunities. Her new work includes founding her own data consulting business, Harris Data Consulting, joining Beeck Center at Georgetown University as a Visiting Fellow, and co-founding and serving as the COO of BrightHive. More than ever, focusing her energy on leveraging the power of data to improve communities across the United States. The goal of BrightHive is to enable States and local governments to responsibly, legally, and securely integrate social sector data that can draw insights, improve outcomes and increase economic opportunities for our most underserved individuals.

Evans Harris is especially interested in the responsible use of data. Just as doctors and lawyers have specific codes of ethics that guide those professionals in their practices, Evans Harris advocates for a similar code of ethics in data science, frameworks, standards, and stronger accountability for ethical practices by all.

"We are just starting to have the urgency conversation on data ethics and responsibility. Things like the European Union's General Data Protection Regulation (GDPR), and the consumer data protection bill in California, are

huge steps forward in giving people more control over how their data is being used." Under, GDPR, companies are required to disclose a privacy policy to their customers. The policy can no longer be something that only a lawyer will understand. The GDPR requires information to be transparent, simple to understand for the intended audience and accessible.

"Putting a small statement that gives companies consent isn't right. People don't even realize what control they are relinquishing over their data. If I can picture the way data is used in the future, I picture everyone understanding and having control over how their data is used. It's not this passive commodity, it's an interactive and active control over how you are represented.

To make this happen, we must also recognize that ethics isn't something just to be enforced; we actually have lots of privacy laws that get violated and then enforced daily. The lack of a standard for ethical behavior is what I consider our greatest challenge. The fact is, you're only as trustworthy and ethical as society says you are and society is just starting to scream, they expect more out of government and the tech community. GDPR and other data protection laws are the right compliance measures to improve ethical practices,

So, what does it look like to responsibly use data and technology to effect social change? That's what I'm focused on today. Through BrightHive, we're showing that you can be a for-profit company, that builds ethical design practices into the entire development process and then measures success by societal impact, rather than corporate profits. Through CPEDS (now Global Data Ethics Project) we showing that everyone can drive change and must be a part of solving the problem. I'm also a Strategic Advisor for a non-profit, Digitally Responsible Aid, who recognize the benefits of digital technologies in our most vulnerable spaces globally but also the risks these technologies can place on individuals in these areas. They focus on equipping humanitarian practitioners with the tool, research and guidance necessary to navigate the intersection of digital and human security. The face of innovation in the future is one that not only maximizes the impact of new technologies, but puts responsible use of data, privacy protection, and consumer empowerment at the ethos of their missions.

Can you provide an example of people having more control over how their data is being used?

"We're starting to see companies like Microsoft and Google recognize the imperative to give consumers more control over their data. Gmail's updates in 2018, for example, give users the ability to have emails expire after a certain amount of time. You'll know companies won't be able to keep your personal data after a specified amount of time, reducing the risk of leaking personal information as a result of a company breach. This shows we are moving in the right direction.

I'd love to put energy into building individual awareness around how data is used. For example, social media data that might get used to determine if you get a job, or a loan. Our society is definitely more data savvy then 10 years ago, but there's still this gap in understanding personal impact that is creating fear and technology backlash. This is where local community organizations can really make a difference. Places like schools or local libraries. We need to meet people where they are, in their own spaces. We can have banks and other organizations speak to the fact that your data is being collected and the implications. Explain to the moms and dads how their (and their children's) digital presence is being used.

We need to have these conversations with our friends and families. One day, we were having a girls' night; we had our kids with us and a friend of mine had her 10-year-old daughter. Her daughter decided to Google herself. She found all of these YouTube videos from when she was 3-4 years old doing gymnastics. She was mortified, she would never want this out there. Something so small became a conversation around her right to control her digital footprint.

Once my husband and I became parents, we had a conversation about how much of our daughter we were willing to put out there. We live in a time where this conversation is just as important as what schools do we choose, what religion do we follow?"

The voice of the people

Natalie Evans Harris is a key leader speaking to the policy issues of large-scale data collection. Through her work at BrightHive, she is trying to engage both the subject matter experts and the public in the discussion about data ethics. The collection of data and the use of data are issues that impact everyone, as evidenced by the latest scandal involving Facebook's use/mis-use of information. Evans Harris is working, just as she did in the government, to empower the public at the lowest levels and to connect the experts so that the field of data science continues to contribute positively to the public good. Although she may no longer be walking the halls of the White House, she continues to serve the American people through her work as an educator and advocate for data science ethics.

What are you focused on for the next few years?

"Responsible data use will continue to be my area of focus. I'm working with academia to see ethics incorporated into more curriculums, to create ethical data scientists. Success is when someone graduates from a data science program and they call themselves a data scientist. They should have their own personal code of ethics for how they will make sure they will responsibly use data. Then, we can start to figure out how to hold each other accountable. I want to see real movement in addressing the political, legal, cultural and technical challenges to government adopting digital services that can improve social service delivery. I want to see ethics in organization – governance frameworks that explicitly say this is how we make sure your data is being used properly. This is how we are protecting your data, securing, and using your data to benefit you and your community. I want an explicit contract like that.

We need to get to a place where when you are faced with a contract agreement to, for example, to download an app in exchange for your data, you can say no to the agreement, still use the app, and not allow others to use your data. We are moving in the right direction now when apps ask if you want to provide access to your location services, or your photos. Informed consent for use of your information should be more than just a check box. We need companies to set the default response of using your data to be a no; right now, the default is yes.

We need to get to a point where everyone in the community is involved and aware. We need these conversations at the dinner table. I want my mom to understand how her data is used."

VIVIAN ZHANG

CTO & CHIEF DATA SCIENTIST OF NYC DATA SCIENCE ACADEMY

"I have recognized the rising importance of data science, the strong need for people to learn and apply the skills in their own field and life."

D o your best every day. This is the challenge that Vivian S. Zhang strives to embody in her role as a prominent data scientist. In the world of data science, where women typically have less representation, Zhang has been the embodiment of a persistent, professional woman.

Why did you choose a career in data?

"In 1997, I intentionally asked my cousin who has deep industrial insights, 'What is the future of computer science?' He responded, 'Data mining that you can do on your own laptop!' That's something that I kept in mind when pursuing my education.

In 2009, I earned a double Masters of Science in Computer Science and Applied Math and Statistics while working on multiple projects. I built up experience in the field through research, consulting, and developing real products, and now I am the founder/CTO of my own analytics consulting firm called SupStat and its subsidiary, NYC Data Science Academy.

NYC Data Science Academy is an educational, training and career development organization that offers a variety of services including full-time bootcamps, part-time courses, corporate training, consulting, and career services. The company is committed to improving the data science community and all of its members.

"I have recognized the rising importance of data science, the strong need for people to learn and apply the skills in their own field and life. It is amazing to witness how much this field has developed over the last 20 years."

Early life and education

Vivian Zhang began her adventure in data science at a relatively young age. She acknowledges that the love of science and mathematics come from her DNA. Her family positively impacted her desire to study those subjects. Before the laptop computer became commonplace, one of Zhang's family members whetted her appetite for information technology when he predicted that individuals in the future would routinely perform data mining on their own laptops. This discussion prompted her to begin learning coding and programming in high school.

Zhang's love of computer science lead her to pursue a Bachelor's of Science degree in Computer Science and two Masters of Science degrees, one in Computer Science and one in Statistics.

Giving back to the community

While Zhang has the formal training necessary for her to succeed in the private sector, she recognizes that many people lack the opportunities that she enjoyed. An enduring theme throughout her career has been the importance of sharing the knowledge that she has been privileged to learn. Much of her work has also focused on using data to provide practical solutions to problems faced by ordinary people.

Her resume includes a diverse array of work. She started with Stony Brook Medicine in September 2008. Her work there consisted of developing algorithms help to improve efficiency. She helped to calculate the costs for different medical services and worked on ways to improve drug safety. Her next position was as a programmer for Brown University. Working with other scholars, Zhang helped sift through data from a Kenyan hospital that specialized in treating patients with HIV. The research was aimed at reducing the cost of the test that determines the viral load of the illness. Testing the viral load of the illness can indicate the effectiveness of the treatment. These tests, which can be costly, should be done frequently after treatment begins, adding another barrier to treating people in portions of the world that face economic challenges.

In February 2012, Zhang made another move to work with the Memorial Sloan-Kettering Cancer Center. Again, much of her work focused on leveraging the power of data to improve health care functions. She used her analysis skills to predict financial and patient health outcomes. She was able to hone predictions concerning patient readmission, and she was able to find solutions to make patient care more affordable. She also worked to analyze the information from her hospital to see how her institution fared compared to others. She compared her institution to others at the state and national levels, focusing especially on the areas of internal clinical information and financial statistics.

The start of entrepreneurship

"I have designed my career path exactly as it happened. I wanted to first work in top schools and research centers with the smartest people in the world on the most challenging problems in society for 3-4 years. That allowed me to work on real-world problems, applying machine learning and other technical skills. I was working at Brown University and Memorial Sloan Kettering Cancer Research Center. That experience gave me on-the-job-training as thorough and rigorous as a PhD program. I started to recruit clients, running a consulting business on the side since 2011. Consequently, it was not too difficult to start my own business in 2013 with a pool of clients."

In 2013, Zhang would trade out her more traditional jobs for something new and fresh. She would become the co-founder and CTO of SupStat Analytics in July of 2013 and, on top of starting SupStat, she would also develop the NYC Data Science Academy, owned by SupStat, in November of 2013. On top of these ambitious projects, Zhang has been lecturing as an adjunct professor at Stony Brook University since October of 2014. Throughout all of these endeavors, she continues to be very involved in volunteer projects.

SupStat Analytics helps to supplement the growing need for the specialized skill set of data scientists. The primary work of SupStat is statistical analysis, visualization, and computing. Zhang started the consulting business because she was so passionate about the use of data. Working as the CTO and Chief Data Scientist of the business, she is especially concerned about the educational portion of the company.

She enjoys taking the practical skills that she uses in consulting and sharing those skills through the NYC Data Science Academy, which operates under the SupStat umbrella.

Zhang serves as the CTO and Chief Data Scientist on the NYC Data Science Academy team. The academy offers some of the most unique data training available in the world. As Zhang has explained in many interviews, there is a gap between the college education and the need for workers in the field of data science. The academy fills the gap, since there is simply no formal training for the skillset available. There is no other place to get the hands-on training that industry needs.

Traditional educational institutions

A driving force behind Zhang's consulting and education business is her belief that it is difficult for traditional educational institutions to adjust rapidly to meet the needs of the changing economy. She points out that courses at universities must be approved well in advance. Often, there is a lag between the appearance of some new topic and the university's ability to train students on that topic. In this way, she thinks that universities are disadvantaged. Their system almost forces the institution to chronically lag behind. She hopes that institutions will begin putting processes in place to shorten the lag.

However, this observation about traditional educational institutions does not mean that she rejects college education. To the contrary, she thinks that college helps individuals explore themselves and can set a basis for future learning. Continuing education after college can fill the gaps by exposing graduates to the latest developments. The college education can be key for teaching students the fundamentals of math, science, and coding. A solid foundation from college can mean that continuing education is easier to digest. Zhang has repeatedly advocated for students to take on the more challenging subjects like math, as those subjects will improve an individual's ability to be quantitative. She also simply values the experience gained by persevering through a difficult task.

"We saw that while more and more universities are offering master's programs, usually the curriculum is not very close to industry needs, and the curriculum update speed is too slow. In order to close the gap, the school side could consider recruiting more instructors with in-field experience and devote more time to developing the curriculum and getting training in teaching and public speaking. Also, it is important to update the content every quarter, revising at least 10-20% to keep up with industry advancements."

Female role model

On top of the general value of a college education, Zhang advocates for girls to study the hard subjects, like mathematics and science. She personally attests that her academic pedigree has given her advantages, and she hopes to encourage girls to go into fields like computer science, math, and statistics. She does acknowledge that part of the dearth of women in the field is due simply to preference – perhaps coding and statistics simply are not the first choice of many women. However, she is encouraged by women making progress in the field. One indicator of the progress is that there are more women in graduate school than men. She challenges girls to learn the hard stuff early. Math and accounting can give girls the confidence they need not only to manage their own finances but to take on more ambitious projects.

Focused on employee training

The coursework offered in programs like the academy's bootcamp takes individuals from the theoretical or foundational knowledge that is gained in the university setting to the practical knowledge needed by employers in the contemporary environment. Zhang does not merely want to do data science for companies, but she also wants to give companies tools to train their employees to do those jobs. Currently, the academy is looking to continue growing and has partnered with organizations in China. Its students come from every corner of the globe.

Growing her business; formation of the academy

Zhang had not originally intended to start an instruction arm of her consulting business, but she taught data science in a meet-up group as a part of her community service. Part of her inspiration to begin the instruction was this very community service. In providing food to the homeless, Zhang also realized that people needed access to education. She thought of ways to provide free instruction on computer science, to include instruction on open-source data. The meet-up group was her vehicle for instruction. As the group grew, companies began requesting her to provide training for their employees. Zhang relates that when her meet-up instruction became popular, she decided to ask companies to sponsor the training. The companies were excited to have their employees gain practical knowledge to bring back to the workplace, and the academy was born.

Zhang admits that she never imagined much of her efforts would focus on instruction. However, she has created a space in the data science field that adds value to both individuals and businesses. She has created an important service to meet the education needs of the field, and, by filling that gap, she is helping to shape the next generation of data scientists. On top of those impressive achievements, she serves as a positive role model for women hoping to work in the industry. Not only does she give advice, but she takes her own advice: do the hard stuff first. Both Zhang and all her students – past, present, and future – are well-served by this advice.

The menu of training opportunities at the academy includes a 12-week "boot camp," training tailored to corporate clients, and weekend classes. The topics of the classes are wide ranging and include R/Python and Hadoop Beginner. The classes are also available in virtual settings as well as traditional, in-person formats. Zhang also takes great pains to ensure that courses are consistently updated, giving students access to cutting-edge information that focuses on open-source software.

Zhang is less concerned with the technical skills that students have before entering the boot camp than she is about their skills at the end of the training. However, she does relate that individuals with less technical backgrounds may experience a steep learning curve as they traverse the boot camp. No matter their level of technical expertise at the beginning, though, individuals will have the technical skills that they need to succeed by the end. To her, hard work and effort trump any lack of technical knowledge.

The Academy often helps individuals with less technical backgrounds transition into more technical positions. However, Zhang stresses that the transition can be made and can be made successfully. While the hiring process for data scientists is very involved (it requires a broad knowledge of several technical subject as well as practical exercises), about 90% of Academy students find employment in the data science field after 6 months. These statistics are not shabby considering that the skill set was named as an occupation only in about 2008. The list of companies that have hired the academy's student include names like IBM Watson, Spotify, Bloomberg, and Goldman Sachs, just to name a few.

What advantages/ disadvantages do you have being a woman in a field that has traditionally been male-dominated?

When asked about her experience as a woman in this field, Zhang does not complain or feel sorry for herself.

"I felt that the fact that there was a very limited number of females in this field in and of itself works as an advantage or disadvantage. As they are relatively rare, female candidates have an advantage in being sought out for technical teams or firms that want to show some gender balance. At the same time, as a minority, females are less willing to share their views and voices compared to men. The historical reason is very obvious. In my generation, about 4-5% women majored in computer science and about 20-30% women majored in applied math/statistics. When you calculated the population with a background in both fields, that amounts to less than 1%! I hope the numbers have improved over the past 10 years."

Her positive attitude shines, as she acknowledges that most people react very positively to her. Her best advice to women is the same advice that she herself has clearly followed throughout her career: work hard.

While she believes that women can progress through their work ethic, Zhang also reaches out to women to offer tools to help them succeed. Zhang gives talks targeted to women at educational institutions and is always open to sharing information with people who are interested in entering the field.

How do you plan to expand your business in the future? What is the next step for you?

"We are expanding in three distinct areas:

1. We are extending our geographical reach, as we are making our online courses accessible in China. We have partnered with one of the biggest TV channels – Shanghai financial channel – to co-host our online course offering.

2. We are expanding our curriculum into the preparatory stage in the K-12 space. Our subsidiary, rising stars school (http://risingstarsschool.com/), is offering future technology, junior data science education to young kids through summer camps and after-school programs.

3. We are making our courses more accessible online and in-person, opening up the possibility of student visas. With ACCET accreditation, we expect to offer international students visas soon and double/triple our students next year. We are doing a lot of preparation 9 months ahead of time to make sure our offerings still keep the same high standard we have been holding since day one."

What legacy do you hope to leave behind for future data scientists?

"I always think it is a team effort to allow us to help nearly 3,000 students (both part-time and full-time students) to learn and make a successful career transition into data science. I am proud of my team!"

How has being a parent changed your career trajectory/ aspirations?

"It's what made me think of educational opportunities for younger kids. Being a mom of a 6-year-old girl and a baby boy made me decide to start new programs for young kids, and the idea eventually grew into the rising star school."

If someone came to you for advice, as they were thinking about starting a career in the data and analytics industry, what advice would you give them?

"Work hard, be humble, and give yourself at least 6 months to learn and practice. Almost everyone can do it. I have helped and witnessed so many people make this transition!"

REFERENCES

References for Bernard Marr

- Hortonworks Inc. (2018). Hortonworks Congratulates 2018 European Data Heroes Award Winners [online]. Available at: https://www.prnewswire.com/news-releases/hortonworks-congratulates-2018-european-data-heroes-award-winners-300631902.html [Accessed 19 Sep. 2018].

- Perry, J. (2018). Embracing Change in the Epoch of AI [online]. Available at: https://www.financialexecutives.org/FEI-Daily/April-2018/Embracing-Change-in-the-Epoch-of-AI.aspx [Accessed 19 Sep. 2018].

- Fields, J. (2017). [online]. Interview with Bernard Marr, speaker, author, advisor. Available at: http://www.onalytica.com/blog/posts/interview-bernard-marr/ [Accessed 19 Sep. 2018].

- Amazon. (2018). Bernard Marr [online]. Available at: https://www.amazon.com/Bernard-Marr/e/B001H6KUSS [Accessed 19 Sep. 2018].

- Marr, B. (2018). Bernard Marr and Co. [online]. Available at: http://bernardmarr.com/ [Accessed 19 Sep. 2018].

- [online]. Available at: https://www.linkedin.com/in/bernard-marr/ [Accessed 19 Sep. 2018].

- Granville, V. (2016). 10 Great Data Science Articles by Bernard Marr [online]. Available at: https://www.datasciencecentral.com/profiles/blogs/10-great-data-science-articles-by-bernard-marr [Accessed 19 Sep. 2018].

- Marr, B. (n.d.). The Intelligent Company: Five Steps to Success with Evidence-Based Management [online]. Available at: https://www.amazon.com/Intelligent-Company-Success-Evidence-Based-Management/dp/0470685956/ref=sr_1_1?s=books&ie=UTF8&qid=1526251925&sr=1-1&keywords=The+Intelligent+company [Accessed 19 Sep. 2018].

- Marr, B. (2015). Big Data: Using SMART Big Data, Analytics and Metrics to Make Better Decisions and Improve Performance [online]. Available at: https://www.amazon.com/Big-Data-Analytics-Decisions-Performance/dp/1118965833/ref=sr_1_1?s=books&ie=UTF8&qid=1526252492&sr=1-1&keywords=big+data+bernard+marr [Accessed 19 Sep. 2018].

References for Carla Gentry

- Gentry, C. (2015). Being a Data Scientist [online]. Available at: https://www.linkedin.com/pulse/being-data-scientist-carla-gentry/ [Accessed 19 Sep. 2018].

- Sharon Fisher 3 Questions With 'Data Nerd' Carla Gentry March 12, 2014

- Eileen Mcnulty Contributors Carla Gentry- Founder and Data Scientist, Analytical Solution· May 21, 2014

- Nerd, A. (n.d.). Let's get real about artificial intelligence and machine learning [online]. Available at: http://analytical-solution.com/ [Accessed 19 Sep. 2018].

- Carla Gentry on Twitter. Available at: https://twitter.com/data_nerd [Accessed 19 Sep. 2018].

- Nerd, A. (n.d.). [online]. Available at: http://analytical-solution.com/ [Accessed 19 Sep. 2018].

- Dataner13. (n.d.). Datanerd13 [online]. Available at: https://www.linkedin.com/in/datanerd13/ [Accessed 19 Sep. 2018].

- Carla Gentry on Linkedin. Transforming Data with Intelligence Las Vegas CONFERENCE February 11–16

- [online]. Available at: https://www.linkedin.com/pulse/all-those-thought-had-failed-carla-gentry/ [Accessed 19 Sep. 2018].

- Gentry, C. (2017). For all those that thought they had failed [online]. Available at: https://www.lascrfiche.com/simplicity/3-questions-data-nerd-carla-gentry/ [Accessed 19 Sep. 2018].

- Metis. (2017). Demystifying Data Science 2017 | Conversation with a Data Scientist | Carla Gentry [online]. Available at: https://www.youtube.com/watch?v=B92nBe-gZV0 [Accessed 19 Sep. 2018].

- Dar, P. (2018). DataHack Radio #4 – Data Privacy, Women in Data Science and More with Carla Gentry [online]. Available at: https://www.analyticsvidhya.com/blog/2018/07/datahack-radio-episode-4-carla-gentry/ [Accessed 19 Sep. 2018].

- Reinstein, I. (2018). Top 10 Active Big Data, Data Science, Machine Learning Influencers on LinkedIn [online]. Available at: https://www.kdnuggets.com/2017/09/top-10-big-data-science-machine-learning-influencers-linkedin-updated.html [Accessed 19 Sep. 2018].

References for Craig Brown

- Beck J. (2016). The Decline of the Driver's License [online]. Available at: https://www.theatlantic.com/technology/archive/2016/01/the-decline-of-the-drivers-license/425169/ [Accessed 19 Sep. 2018].

- Brown, C. (2016). Meet Craig [online]. Available at: http://www.craigbrownphd.com/about-me/ [Accessed 19 Sep. 2018].

- Humans of Analytics. (2017). Craig Brown: Technology Maven, Analytics Influencer, and Avid Rider [online]. Available at: http://humansofanalytics.com/craig-brown-phd-technology-analytics-influencer/ [Accessed 19 Sep. 2018].

- Wysocki Jr., B. (1996). Flying Solo [online]. Available at: http://www.craigbrownphd.com/wp-content/uploads/2012/09/Flying-Solo-High-Tech-Nomads-Write-New-Program-For-Future-of-Work.jpg [Accessed 19 Sep. 2018].

- [online]. Available at: https://www.linkedin.com/in/craigbrownphd/ [Accessed 19 Sep. 2018].

- National BDPA. (n.d.). About us [online]. Available at: http://www.bdpa.org/?page=About_Us [Accessed 19 Sep. 2018].

- Albertson, M. (2018). Beyond the AI hype: Experts weigh in on AI growing pains, modern use cases [online]. Available at: https://siliconangle.com/blog/2018/03/02/beyond-ai-hype-experts-weigh-ai-growing-pains-modern-use-cases-ibmml/ [Accessed 19 Sep. 2018].

- Data. (2018). Craig Brown - Humans of Data Science [online]. Available at: https://www.youtube.com/watch?v=mdqsPB9btDo [Accessed 19 Sep. 2018].

References for DP Patil

- Hiler, K. (2016). An Exit Interview With U.S. Chief Data Scientist DJ PatilAvailable at: https://www.sciencefriday.com/segments/an-exit-interview-with-u-s-chief-data-scientist-dj-patil/ [Accessed 19 Sep. 2018].

- Recode. (2018). Full transcript: Chief Data Scientist DJ Patil of the U.S. Office of Science and Technology Policy on Recode Decode [online]. Available at: https://www.recode.net/2016/12/28/14106602/full-transcript-chief-data-scientist-dj-patil-science-technology-policy [Accessed 19 Sep. 2018].

- Wikipedia Contributors. (2018). DJ Patil [online]. Available at: https://en.wikipedia.org/wiki/DJ_Patil [Accessed 19 Sep. 2018].

- Bereznak, A. (2015). Meet DJ Patil: Obama's Big Data dude [online]. Available at: https://www.yahoo.com/news/meet-dj-patil-obamas-big-data-dude-deputy-chief-115849466441.html [Accessed 19 Sep. 2018].

- Berkeley School of Information. (2013). DJ Patil: Commencement 2013 keynote speaker [online]. Available at: https://www.youtube.com/watch?v=cbiuJCDtu3E

- [online]. Available at: https://www.linkedin.com/in/dpatil/ [Accessed 19 Sep. 2018].

References for Drew Conway

- Conway, D. & White, J. (2012). Machine Learning for Hackers: Case Studies and Algorithms to Get You Started [online]. Available at: http://shop.oreilly.com/product/0636920018483.do [Accessed 19 Sep. 2018].

- Drew Conway Data Consulting. (2015). The Data Science Venn Diagram [online]. Available at: http://drewconway.com/zia/2013/3/26/the-data-science-venn-diagram [Accessed 19 Sep. 2018].

- Conway, D. (2011). Machine Learning for Email: Spam Filtering and Priority Inbox [online]. Available at: https://www.

amazon.com/Machine-Learning-Email-Filtering-Priority/
dp/1449314309[Accessed 19 Sep. 2018].

- Data Science Pioneer Drew Conway Closes $2.5M in Seed
  Funding to Bring Machine Learning to Industrial Operations

- Johnston, L. (2018). Data Science Pioneer Drew Conway Closes $2.5M in Seed Funding to Bring Machine Learning to Indus-
  trial Operations [online]. Available at: https://globenewswire.
  com/news-release/2016/12/07/969387/0/en/Data-Science-
  Pioneer-Drew-Conway-Closes-2-5M-in-Seed-Funding-to-
  Bring-Machine-Learning-to-Industrial-Operations.html[Ac-
  cessed 19 Sep. 2018].

- Simply Statistics. (2012). Interview with Drew Conway - Author of "Machine Learning for Hackers" [online]. Available
  at: https://simplystatistics.org/2012/04/13/interview-with-
  drew-conway-author-of-machine/ [Accessed 19 Sep. 2018].

- Johnston, L. (2016). Data Science Pioneer Drew Conway Closes $2.5M in Seed Funding to Bring Machine Learning to In-
  dustrial Operations [online]. Available at: https://globenews-
  wire.com/news-release/2016/12/07/969387/0/en/Data-
  Science-Pioneer-Drew-Conway-Closes-2-5M-in-Seed-Fund-
  ing-to-Bring-Machine-Learning-to-Industrial-Operations.html
  [Accessed 19 Sep. 2018].

- Wolfe, J. (2016). Using Data Science For The Physical
  World [online]. Available at: https://www.forbes.com/sites/
  joshwolfe/2016/03/03/using-data-science-for-the-physi-
  cal-world/#26cfdc7d150e[Accessed 19 Sep. 2018].

- Conway, D. (2010). The Data Science Venn Diagram [online].
  Available at: http://www.dataists.com/2010/09/the-data-sci-
  ence-venn-diagram/ [Accessed 19 Sep. 2018].

- Johnston, L. (2016). Data Science Pioneer Drew Conway Closes $2.5M in Seed Funding to Bring Machine Learning to Industrial Operations [online]. Available at: http://www.marketwired.com/press-release/data-science-pioneer-drew-conway-closes-25m-seed-funding-bring-machine-learning-industrial-2181338.htm [Accessed 19 Sep. 2018].

- DataKind. (2015). Our Story [online]. Available at: http://www.datakind.org/our-story [Accessed 19 Sep. 2018].

References for Kirk Borne

- Howell, E. (2017). Challenger: Shuttle Disaster That Changed NASA [online]. [online]. Available at: https://www.space.com/18084-space-shuttle-challenger.html [Accessed 19 Sep. 2018].

- Big Data is a Big Deal. [online]. Available at: https://obamawhitehouse.archives.gov/blog/2012/03/29/big-data-big-deal [Accessed 19 Sep. 2018].

- Borne, K. (2015). A Growth Hacker's Journey – At the right place at the right time [online]. Available at: https://mapr.com/blog/growth-hackers-journey-right-place-right-time/ [Accessed 19 Sep. 2018].

- [online]. Available at: https://obamawhitehouse.archives.gov/blog/2012/03/29/big-data-big-deal [Accessed 19 Sep. 2018].

- Kalil, T. (2012). Big Data is a Big Deal [online]. Available at: https://www.linkedin.com/in/kirkdborne/ [Accessed 19 Sep. 2018].

- Vaughan, J. (2015). Kirk Borne on data science and big data analytics, data literacy [online]. Available at: https://search-datamanagement.techtarget.com/feature/Kirk-Borne-on-data-science-and-big-data-analytics-data-literacy [Accessed 19 Sep. 2018].

- [online]. Available at: https://www.datascienceweekly.org/data-scientist-interviews/data-mining-nasa-data-science-teaching-gmu-kirk-borne-interview [Accessed 19 Sep. 2018].

- Data Science Weekly. (2016). Data Mining at NASA to Teaching Data Science at GMU: Kirk Borne Interview [online]. Available at: https://www.space.com/18084-space-shuttle-challenger.html [Accessed 19 Sep. 2018].

- Boland, S. (2018). The Data Incubator. (2018). Data Science in 30 Minutes: Kirk Borne – A Fortuitous Career in Data Science [online]. Available at: https://blog.thedataincubator.com/2018/01/ds30-kirk-borne/ [Accessed 19 Sep. 2018].

- The Arts and Entertainment Magazine. (n.d.). TAEM Interview with Dr. Kirk Borne of George Mason University [online]. Available at: http://eeriedigest.com/2013/01/taem-interview-with-dr-kirk-borne-of-george-mason-university/ [Accessed 19 Sep. 2018].

References for Mico Yuk

- SAP Anaylitics. (2016). Mico Yuk on Reimagine Analytics: The Time Is Now [online]. Available at: https://www.youtube.com/watch?v=nk5j2ViZxrs [Accessed 19 Sep. 2018].

- Mico Yuk Explains How BI Storyboards Can Increase User Buy-In: https://www.youtube.com/watch?v=JZF0lpV6yHk&t=1020s

- How to Build Actionable KPIs | Business Intelligence | Data Analytics: https://www.youtube.com/watch?v=MUKY-41PU28c&t=19s

- 2017 State of the Black Tech Ecosystem [Livestream]: https://youtu.be/ewi46bVRzak?t=1964

- Klipfolio. (2018). Dashboard Examples [online]. Available at: https://www.klipfolio.com/resources/dashboard-examples/supply-chain [Accessed 19 Sep. 2018].

- Payne, K. (2018). Dashboard Examples [online]. Available at: https://looker.com/blog/women-of-data-mico-yuk [Accessed 19 Sep. 2018].

- Yasteq. (n.d.). Black Tech Mecca [online]. Available at: https://www.yasteq.com/US/Chicago/369002126616240/Black-Tech-Mecca [Accessed 19 Sep. 2018].

- Yuk, M. (n.d.). Micko Yuk [online]. Available at: http://micoyuk.com/ [Accessed 19 Sep. 2018].

- BI Brainz. (n.d.). About the Author: Mico Yuk [online]. Available at: http://bibrainz.com/aof/author/micoyuk/ [Accessed 19 Sep. 2018].

- BI Brainz. (2016). BI Dashboard Formula Methodology: How to make your first big data visualization in any tool [online]. Available at: https://www.slideshare.net/bibrainz/how-to-make-your-first-big-data-visualization [Accessed 19 Sep. 2018].

- 2018 Experian Information Solutions. (2018). The Art & Science of Creating Intelligent Data Visualizations w/ @MicoYuk #DataTalk [online]. Available at: http://www.experian.com/blogs/news/datatalk/intelligent-data-visualizations/ [Accessed 19 Sep. 2018].

- Yuk, M. (2018). 11 Reasons Why Most Business Intelligence Projects Fail

- Mico Yuk discusses what companies can do [online]. Available at: https://channels.theinnovationenterprise.com/articles/11-reasons-why-most-business-intelligence-projects-fail [Accessed 19 Sep. 2018].

References for Monica Rogati

- LinkedIn. (2018). Monica Rogati [online]. Available at: https://www.linkedin.com/in/mrogati/ [Accessed 19 Sep. 2018].

- Wikipedia Contributors. (2018). Monica Rogati [online]. Available at: https://en.wikipedia.org/wiki/Monica_Rogati [Accessed 19 Sep. 2018].

- O'Reilly. (2011). Strata Summit 2011: Monica Rogati, "Lies, Damned Lies, and the Data Scientist" [online]. Available at: https://www.youtube.com/watch?v=gIXoPT-uWu0 [Accessed 19 Sep. 2018].

- Woods, D. (2011). LinkedIn's Monica Rogati On "What is a Data Scientist?" [online]. Available at: https://www.forbes.com/sites/danwoods/2011/11/27/linkedins-monica-rogati-on-what-is-a-data-scientist/#2a2891933e15 [Accessed 19 Sep. 2018].

- Industry Dive. (2018). 10 Big Data experts to follow on Twitter [online]. Available at: https://www.ciodive.com/news/10-big-data-experts-to-follow-on-twitter/514825/ [Accessed 19 Sep. 2018].

- The Financial Brand. (2018). Artificial Intelligence Needs a Strong Data Foundation [online]. Available at: https://thefinancialbrand.com/67039/ai-hierarchy-of-data-needs/ [Accessed 19 Sep. 2018].

- Novet, J. (2014). LinkedIn had one of the first data science teams. Now it's breaking up the band [online]. Available at:

https://venturebeat.com/2014/10/31/linkedin-data-science-team/ [Accessed 19 Sep. 2018].

- First Round Review. (n.d.). This Is How You Build Products for the New Generation of 'Data Natives' [online]. Available at: http://firstround.com/review/this-is-how-you-build-products-for-the-new-generation-of-data-natives/ [Accessed 19 Sep. 2018].

- Rogati, M. (2011). Easy test for CS PhDs deciding on academia vs. industry: When a simple method works, do you a) curse or b) celebrate? [online]. Available at: https://twitter.com/mrogati/status/85480609803272192 [Accessed 19 Sep. 2018].

- Rogati, M. (2017). How do I become a data scientist? [online]. Available at: https://medium.com/@mrogati/how-do-i-become-a-data-scientist-f8074232608e [Accessed 19 Sep. 2018].

References for Natalie Evans Harris

- O'Reilly Media. (20188). Strata Data Conference Schedule [online]. Available at: https://conferences.oreilly.com/strata/strata-ca/public/schedule/speaker/305158 [Accessed 19 Sep. 2018].

- Australian Alliance for Data Leadership. (n.d.). Speaker Stories: Natalie Evans Harris [online]. Available at: https://www.iapa.org.au/events/2017/advancing-analytics/speaker-stories/natalie-evans-harris [Accessed 19 Sep. 2018].

- Zimmerman, E. (2017). Dispatch from VentureCrushAV: Pulitzer-Winner Joann Lublin on Women Ascending the Corporate Ladder [online]. Available at: https://www.forbes.com/sites/edwardzimmerman/2017/07/18/dispatch-from-venturecrushav-pulitzer-winner-joann-lublin-on-women-ascending-the-corporate-ladder/#521db40029da [Accessed 19 Sep. 2018].

- Schaack, M. (2016). 5 Things to Consider as Government Becomes More Data-Driven [online]. Available at: https://www.govloop.com/5-things-consider-government-becomes-data-driven/ [Accessed 19 Sep. 2018].

- [online]. Available at: https://www.linkedin.com/in/nevan-sharris/ [Accessed 19 Sep. 2018].

- Duckett, C. (2013). Dispatch from VentureCrushAV: Pulitzer-Winner Joann Lublin on Women Ascending the Corporate Ladder [online]. Available at: https://www.zdnet.com/article/nsa-hunger-demands-29-petabytes-of-data-a-day/ [Accessed 19 Sep. 2018].

- Personal Democracy Forum. (2018). Natalie Evans Harris [online]. Available at: https://www.pdf-18.com/speaker/natalie-evans-harris/ [Accessed 19 Sep. 2018].

- Wikipedia Contributors. (2018). Cyber Intelligence Sharing and Protection Act [online]. Available at: https://en.wikipedia.org/wiki/Cyber_Intelligence_Sharing_and_Protection_Act [Accessed 19 Sep. 2018].

- Open Skills Project [online]. Available at: http://dataatwork.org/data/ [Accessed 19 Sep. 2018].

- Australian Alliance for Data Leadership. (n.d.). Speaker Stories: Natalie Evans Harris [online]. Available at: https://www.iapa.org.au/events/2017/advancing-analytics/speaker-stories/natalie-evans-harris [Accessed 19 Sep. 2018].

- The White House. (2016). FACT SHEET: The Opportunity Project – Unleashing the power of open data to build stronger ladders of opportunity for all Americans [online]. Available at: https://obamawhitehouse.archives.gov/the-press-office/2016/10/06/fact-sheet-opportunity-project-unleashing-power-open-data-build [Accessed 19 Sep. 2018].

- Data for Democracy. (2018). Code of Ethics [online]. Available at: http://datafordemocracy.org/projects/ethics.html [Accessed 19 Sep. 2018].

- Erickson, L. C., Harris, N. E., & Lee, M. M. (2018). It's Time to Talk About Data Ethics [online]. Available at: https://www.datascience.com/blog/data-ethics-for-data-scientists [Accessed 19 Sep. 2018].

- Bloomberg. (2017). Bloomberg, BrightHive, And Data For Democracy Launch Initiative To Develop Data Science Code Of Ethics [online]. Available at: https://www.prnewswire.com/news-releases/bloomberg-brighthive-and-data-for-democracy-launch-initiative-to-develop-data-science-code-of-ethics-300524958.html [Accessed 19 Sep. 2018].

- Jordan, B. (1976). 1976 Democratic National Convention Keynote Address [online]. Available at: https://awpc.cattcenter.iastate.edu/2017/03/21/1976-democratic-national-convention-keynote-address-july-12-1976/ [Accessed 19 Sep. 2018].

- Natalie Evans Harris. [online]. Available at: https://harrisdata.squarespace.com/ [Accessed 19 Sep. 2018].

- Data.world. (n.d.). Community Principles on Ethical Data Practices [online]. Available at: https://datapractices.org/community-principles-on-ethical-data-sharing/ [Accessed 19 Sep. 2018].

References for Vivian Zhang

- Zhang, V. (2017). Inspirational Woman Interview: Vivian Zhang [online]. Available at: http://heragenda.com/power-agenda/power-agenda-vivian-zhang/ [Accessed 19 Sep. 2018].

- [online]. Available at: https://inspirationalwomenseries. org/2017/12/15/inspirational-woman-interview-vivian-zhang/ [Accessed 19 Sep. 2018].

- [online]. Available at: https://www.linkedin.com/in/shangxuanzhang/ [Accessed 19 Sep. 2018].

- Wagner, V. (2018). Vivian Zhang [online]. Available at: https://www.technewsworld.com/story/85058.html [Accessed 19 Sep. 2018].

- Data Science Academy. (2018). Vivian Zhang [online]. Available at: https://nycdatascience.com/instructors/vivian-zhang/ [Accessed 19 Sep. 2018].

- Supstat. (n.d.). Consulting [online]. Available at: http://supstat.com/consulting/ [Accessed 19 Sep. 2018].

About the Author

Kate Strachnyi is the author of *Journey to Data Scientist*, which is essentially a compilation of interviews that Kate herself conducted with over 20 amazing data scientists — with backgrounds ranging from LinkedIn and Pinterest to Bloomberg and IBM. She is also the creator of Humans of Data Science (HoDS) - a project that works on showing the human side of data science (housed on her Story by Data YouTube channel).

Kate is a manager working for Deloitte, currently working in the data visualization & reporting space. She previously served as an insights strategy manager and research analyst, where she was responsible for enabling the exchange of information in an efficient and timely manner. Prior to working with data, she focused on risk management, governance, and regulatory response solutions for financial services organizations.

Before joining the consulting world, she worked for the chief risk officer of a full-service commercial bank, where she was in charge of developing an ERM program, annual submission of ICAAP, and gap analysis of Basel II/III directives. Additionally, she worked as a business development associate at the Global Association of Risk Professionals (GARP).

Kate received a Bachelor of Business Administration in Finance and Investments from Baruch College, Zicklin School of Business. Certifications include Project Management Professional (PMP) and Tableau Desktop 10 Qualified Associate.

E-mail: kate@storybydata.com

LinkedIn: https://www.linkedin.com/in/kate-strachnyi-data/

Twitter: @StoryByData

Blog: http://storybydata.com/

YouTube: Story by Data